Science

Progress Papers

1

Answer Book

A J and M D Thomas

Nelson

Thomas Nelson and Sons Ltd
Nelson House Mayfield Road
Walton-on-Thames Surrey
KT12 5PL UK

51 York Place
Edinburgh
EH1 3JD UK

Nelson Blackie
Wester Cleddens Road
Bishopbriggs
Glasgow
G64 2NZ UK

Thomas Nelson (Hong Kong) Ltd
Toppan Building 10/F
22A Westlands Road
Quarry Bay Hong Kong

Distributed in Australia by

Thomas Nelson Australia
102 Dodds Street
South Melbourne
Victoria 3205 Australia

First published by Thomas Nelson and Sons Ltd 1990

ISBN 0-17-423108-3 } Pupils' Book
NPN 9 8 7 6 5 4 3 2

ISBN 0-17-423109-1 } Answer Book
NPN 9 8 7 6 5 4 3

Printed and bound in Great Britain by
Ebenezer Baylis & Son Ltd, Worcester, and London

CONTENTS

NOTES TO TEACHERS, PARENTS AND PUPILS

Notes to teachers and parents

1 Science surrounds today's children and is as much part of their life as numerical skills or the spoken or written word. Just as our thoughts cannot be expressed or discussed until we have the basic skills of language, science cannot be understood without a basic grasp of the ideas and vocabulary of science.

2 These papers are designed to develop the scientific literacy of children between the ages of 10 and 12 by exposing them to the vocabulary and the ways of thinking of the scientific community in an interesting and relaxed way. The papers cover a large proportion of the **National Curriculum** which places Science alongside English language and mathematics as a core subject, and they also provide valuable preparation for the **Common Entrance** examination.
The papers have not been divided into the subject areas physics, chemistry and biology as some contain a mixture of two or three subjects, and some are dedicated to just one. It should be clear from the title of each paper which topics are covered.

3 The papers are not intended just for schoolwork but aim to give pleasure to both parents and children who want to explore the fascinating world of science together at home. (Some of the experiments described are not suitable for children to perform unsupervised.)

4 The questions are not meant solely for assessment purposes, but are also a means of illuminating the text and asking for an observational response. Some of them are open-ended questions which are not appropriate for right/wrong answers, while others have a range of possible answers. Nevertheless, how a student scores on a paper will indicate how well the topic has been understood and will enable you to measure progress.

Instructions to pupils

(a) Read each paper carefully, taking as long as you need to understand what has been discussed.
(b) Read the questions carefully and look for the answer first in the discussion which comes before it in the paper.
(c) Where possible try to find out the answer by performing an experiment. (It is best to perform experiments only when a teacher or parent is present.) Some experiments are suggested – you might think of others for yourself.
(d) Look for the answer in books – others may have discovered it before you.
(e) Never be afraid to ask other people for help.
(f) If you find it difficult to express the answer to some questions in words, draw a diagram to convey your meaning. There is often space in the text.

REMEMBER! If you don't know the answer to a question, do as scientists have always done – observe, experiment, record and read what others have discovered before you.

A. J. T.

PAPER 1 WHAT IS SCIENCE?

This paper is designed to introduce you to some of the ideas of science. It will help you to work as scientists work, and to think as they think.

Scientists are looking for truth; watch out for things in this paper that are not true!

Lucy teaches Linus some science!

[1–10]
In this song Lucy is teaching her little brother Linus some "Little known facts".

'Do you see this tree? It is a fir tree. It's called a fir tree because it gives us fur, for coats, It also gives us wool in the wintertime.

This is an elm tree. It's very little, But it will grow up into a giant tree, An oak! You can tell how old it is by counting its leaves.

And 'way up there, Those fluffy little white things, Those are clouds; They make the wind blow. And 'way down there, those tiny little black things; Those are bugs! They make the grass grow . . . . They run around all day long, tugging and tugging at each tiny seedling until it grows into a great tall blade of grass.'

Most of us reading or hearing this song would get an uncomfortable feeling that somehow Lucy had got a few things wrong. She is trying to explain to Linus her understanding of a few things. Unfortunately, Lucy is not very accurate.

1 How many mistakes has Lucy made in what she tells Linus? Seven

2 Would Lucy make a good scientist? No

3 – 4 What do you think are two of her main faults? Confusion and inaccuracy
(Also, she doesn't check her information, she passes off opinions as facts.)

How could Lucy teach Linus some better known facts about fir trees, fur coats, wool, clouds, and grass? Are the following suggestions useful? If so, mark with a **U**. If not mark with an **N**.

5 She could ask various people. U

6 She could look for information in books or libraries. U

7 She could read expert opinions. U

8 She could check some of the information herself by observation. U

9 She could check through computer databases to see if they contain information on any of her subjects. U

10 She could check all of the information by observation. N

[11–16]
In past times, people held many ideas which we now believe to be untrue or inaccurate.

In the late 16th century, it was still believed that the earth was flat, and that if you sailed over the horizon, you would fall off the earth.

Most people in the civilised world now agree that the world is round, and the "Flat Earth Society" is considered comical. As better instruments for navigation were developed and the world was explored, it became more and more clear to sailors and astronomers that the world must be round. And when flight and space exploration became possible we could see for ourselves.

Much of our scientific knowledge comes in the form of little bits and pieces that are put together until the picture becomes clear.

First someone questions something. Then someone asks another question, and finds an answer that gives a better explanation.

This answer is then used to suggest what might happen in another situation.

This is called a **theory** or **hypothesis**, and scientists spend all their working lives looking for clearer theories to explain the world and its happenings, and testing these answers to see how accurate they are.

In the past, as information was gathered, it was remembered, or when human language developed it was passed on from one human memory to another.

As the amount of information became too great for individual memories, records began to be kept. People used sticks on which they carved notches to keep count of something, carved tablets and written records or books. Now we have filmed and taped records, and computer databases.

We cannot know all there is to know at any one time, but working theories and hypotheses help us to fit together a pattern of how things happen.

Say whether you think the following statements are **true or false** by underlining the correct answer:

11 Primitive people were always wrong in their explanations of things. (true, false)

12 You cannot use a tool without understanding exactly how it works. (true, false)

13 You can probably make a better tool if you understand how it works. (true, false)

14 Everything printed in books must be correct, because it is carefully checked. (true, false)

15 Scientists can explain how everything in the world works. (true, false)

16 Putting information into a computer is the most accurate way of storing it. (true, false)

A little bit of history

[17–20]
Let us look at some of the scientific discoveries of the past to see how knowledge developed.

People four hundred years ago wore spectacles with glass lenses. These helped those with poor eyesight, especially when reading by candle or oil lamp.

By the 17th century some Dutchmen started using lenses in different combinations, to make the first microscopes and telescopes.

In Italy, Galileo, a scientist very interested in the study of the skies, or **astronomy**, heard of these developments, and used lenses to make his own telescopes.

He built some which could magnify up to 30 times and used them to look at the stars.

For the first time, instead of just seeing twinkling spots of light in the sky he was able to see the planets in detail. Galileo saw the rings of Saturn and the moons of Jupiter as well as details of our own moon.

17 What were glass lenses first used for? Spectacles, improving poor vision

18 How are the microscope and telescope similar? They both magnify objects

19 What are the differences between a microscope and a telescope?

Microscopes help us to see small nearby objects. Telescopes help us to see distant objects.

20 Astronomy is the study of (the universe, how the stars affect our lives, how one navigates according to the stars, the earth and other planets). Underline the correct answers.

[21–24]
Before Galileo, people believed that the Earth was the very centre of the Universe. He showed that this belief was wrong. In fact, Earth was one of several planets which revolved around the sun, which was the central star of one particular system.

Although Galileo's observations enabled him to make some of the most important discoveries in science, he got into trouble with some of the authorities of his time.

They believed, without scientific proof, that God had placed our Earth at the centre of the Universe. It was a long time before these ideas were forgotten.

Galileo made many measurements of the stars, the sun, the moon and the earth. He recorded their movements in the sky and their relationship to each other over a very long time. Eventually he started to see patterns which repeated themselves.

Although Galileo used his imagination to produce ideas on gravity, and astronomy, he could not have made some of his most important discoveries without the development of necessary tools like the telescope, so that he could actually 'see' what was happening.

He also needed the mathematical skills to form his many observations into a simple mathematical formula which he could use to explain to other interested scientists just what he thought was happening in the universe.

21 Many people in Galileo's world believed that (the sun was a god, the earth was the centre of the universe, there was only one moon, there was only one sun, Galileo's ideas were dangerous). Underline the one that is *not* true.

22 What did Galileo discover about the earth? It revolved around the sun

23 Major discoveries in science often depend on other important discoveries or inventions. (true, false)

24 Recording the movements of the sun, moon and earth for long periods enabled Galileo to discover that the moon revolved around the earth and the earth revolved around the sun

[25–30]

In prehistoric times, people who lived near rivers felt the need to explore and travel. With no other means than walking, the opportunity to use the river and its waters must have been very appealing. Watching logs float down the river gave these early people ideas for their own transport.

Perhaps someone long forgotten, decided to hollow out a log, sit in it, and use a pole to steer and paddle along, making one of the earliest boats: the dugout. Or, maybe the floating logs reminded them of something else, and they decided to tie several logs together with vines to make the first raft.

25 What do you think would have been the major problem with just sitting on a log? It would easily overbalance

26 Would hollowing out the log have helped? Yes, sitting in it would be more stable

27 What might have been used to paddle and steer before the pole was thought of? Sticks, branches or even hands

28 What advantage would the raft have over a dugout? It would be much more stable and carry heavier loads

29 What advantage would the dugout have over a raft? It would be easier to paddle and steer

30 Science and invention proceed (in small steps, in giant leaps, a combination of both). Underline the best answer.

[31–33]

The French scientist Ampère is honoured for his discoveries about electricity. The ampere, or amp, the universally accepted name for the unit of electric current, is named after him. He was the first scientist to look methodically into the relationship between magnetism and electricity.

Ampère set out a way of looking at and investigating scientific matters which is still basic to what many scientists do today.

He realised that everything that we know depends on the information which we receive through our senses.

When we see a flower we see the results of a 'message' from the flower through our eyes to our brain.

When we remember what a flower looks like, we receive a message from our brain, even when the flower is no longer there to be seen.

Ampère understood that even though some things could not be 'seen', one could imagine that they existed, to explain events that one *could* see and measure.

For example, you never 'see' an electric current. You 'see' the light it produces, 'feel' the heat it produces in a radiant heater, 'hear' the music it produces in a radio, or a record-player, 'see' the movement of a needle on a measuring instrument. Therefore it is reasonable to believe that an electric current exists.

In the same way, scientists suggested that all things were made up of molecules or atoms. No one was able to see these molecules or atoms, but the scientists developed a theory which explained the way that substances behaved, based upon this suggestion.

If everything were made of atoms, then the ways in which these atoms were grouped decided the molecules that things were made from. These groupings and connections decided how materials behaved.

The whole science of chemistry was founded on this supposition or **prediction**.

Today, we can actually see molecules with an electron microscope, but they existed in imagination long before they were proved to exist in reality.

31 On a still day can you experience air with your senses? Not easily

32 How do you know that air exists? You can feel the wind blow

33 How can you prove that air exists? You can make a draught with a fan and watch papers fluttering

[34–38]
Long before people called themselves 'scientists', there were many who were curious about what was happening in the world about them.

Fill in the gaps with these words:

lunar year tides month phases

Ancient peoples kept records of the ....phases.... of the moon which gave them the ....lunar.... calendar. They also may have noticed that the ....tides.... of the sea varied regularly with the different phases of the moon, at different times of the ....month.... as well as at different times of the ....year....

When something is important to people, they take notice, start to collect information and ask questions. The questions that are asked, and the way in which they are asked, will often decide how useful the answers will be.

When we want to know something, we become **selective**. In other words, we choose to notice very special bits of information, and decide to discard most of what we consider unimportant for answering our question.

If we throw away information which is very important, because we do not realise that we need it, we will probably miss finding our answers.

If you are going to be a good scientist, you will have to ask the right questions, design good, fair tests and select the most useful answers.

Information and measurement

[39–45]
All living things, from the simplest to the most complex (which is man), gather information through their senses. We know about the five main human senses which are:

39 ....sight....　**40** ....hearing....　**41** ....smell....

42 ....taste....　**43** ....touch....

But how does a plant sense or react to its surroundings? The needs of a plant are relatively simple. It requires light to provide energy, and it needs water and dissolved minerals.

44 How would a plant react to light, if, for example, it was growing on a windowsill?

....Its leaves would grow towards the light....

45 How would you expect a plant to react when it cannot get all the water it needs?

....Its roots would grow towards moisture....

[46–50]
Science is concerned with 'exact measurement'. Guesses and imaginative ideas alone are not enough.

In fact, 'exact measurement' is an idea which needs looking at very carefully.

Why should we want to measure something at all? It might be just curiosity. More frequently it is a concern with our well-being which starts most collections of measurements.

When people lived in caves, they soon noticed the difference between night and day, the seasons of the year, and the weather conditions that were best for hunting or fishing.

Hunters would have rapidly learned that when animals were down-wind so that their scent blew towards the animal, they were much less successful than when the animals were up-wind and less able to sense them.

When pre-historic folk began to farm, they must have continually noticed which climates and weather conditions best rewarded them with good crops. They would have learned quickly to notice the point in the growth of crops when plentiful water was important, and a drought disastrous.

So people learned to measure time, distance, direction and amounts.

Measuring, then, starts when people want to be precise about what is happening in a certain event, so that they can begin to say what will make that event happen again, or know what sort of conditions usually accompany it.

When we measure something, we look at it, listen to it, touch it, taste it or smell it. We can do this ourselves, or use an instrument or instruments to do the measuring.

A scale is important. A scale of time, amount or intensity can be measured and compared.

46 Is a ruler a measuring instrument? Yes

47 A thermometer is an instrument that measures temperature

48 A clock or watch measures time

49 A weathervane measures wind direction

50 How could the temperature marked on a thermometer be checked? By comparing them with known temperatures such as the freezing and boiling points of water.

[51–58]
Fill in the blanks in the following paragraphs using words from this list:

specific experiments use precise time sufficient precision measurements

Depending on how important something is, the measurements will be broad and general, or refined and detailed.

Snow and ice are very important in Eskimos' lives. They have dozens of words to describe very specific kinds of snow and ice. Eskimos, because of their need can describe snow and ice in a precise way, while we in Britain need only to recognise that snow and ice are cold, usually wet and always slippery.

We place great importance on the measurement of time in our society, and measure the amount of time by hundredths of a second for some sporting events, while some physics experiments require time to be measured in millionths of a second.

Some societies are content to measure time only by day and night, phases of the moon and seasons of the year, and that is all that is necessary for the way they live.

The precision needed for a measurement depends on the use to which it will put. To decide who is the fastest runner over 100 metres requires time to be measured to a hundredth of a second, but in judging the age of trees it is often sufficient for time to be measured to the nearest year.

[59–67]
According to the old system of measuring length, a foot was equal to about 12 inches, or in metric units, nearly 30 centimetres. A horse is still measured in 'hands', we say that a horse is 14, or 15, or 16, hands high. A 'hand' was originally the width of an adult's palm.

What do the above measurements tell you about the origins of early measures of length or height?

59 What does the length of the foot tell you? It was based on the length of (a man's foot, a woman's foot, a child's foot). Underline the best answer.

60 Was the foot an exact measurement when it was first used? (Yes, no, probably not.) Underline the best answer.

61 Was it useful? Yes

62 Both the 'foot' and the 'hand' started out as rough/coarse/approximate measurements,

63 and both became more exact measurements as people became more sophisticated.

64 Once we start measuring things or events, we begin to look for those which are unique or repeated, in order to begin to see what patterns emerge.

65 If we are studying a disease, we tend to look for those things which are (unique to the ill, shared with everyone) Underline the best answer.

Sometimes people think that all measurements must be as precise as possible. In fact an approximate measurement may sometimes be as useful.

66 For example, if we know that a 'hand' (the width of a palm) is roughly 4 inches or 10 centimetres, then if we also know that most horses are 14–16 hands high, then we can give an approximate range for the height of most horses from 140 centimetres to 160 centimetres.

67 Special breeds of horses, such as Shires, can stand 17–18 hands high, and are therefore roughly 1.7 to 1.8 metres high, while Ponies are 13 hands high at the most and are often considerably smaller.

[68–75]
Fill in the blanks in the following paragraphs using these words:

relate learning brain store discover explanation know information

Sometimes when measuring or studying one thing, scientists or investigators suddenly discover something very important about something else.
Scientists should always be trying to relate what they are learning to all the things they already know
This is one of the most important qualities of a scientist. They organise their perception and their measurements in terms of whatever 'hypothesis' or explanation they are working on, but at the same time constantly store their bits of information, in their brain as well as in their computer so that they can try out different ideas, and ways of organising the information

The earth in space

The sun, the stars and the planets

[1–5]
Human beings have always gazed in wonder at the sky. Early man soon recognised the importance of the **sun, moon and planets** and, not understanding them, worshipped them as gods.

They soon began to see that these moved with great regularity and used them to measure time and form the basis of their calendars.

On a clear night, away from the lights of the town or city, you can see a very large number of **stars** that appear as tiny pinpoints of light. Although they seem so small, we now know that stars are very large spherical objects that are enormously hot and bright. They appear so tiny because they are so far away.

The distances in the universe are so great that it is very inconvenient to describe them in kilometres because the numbers get so big.

Astronomers usually measure distance in **light years**. A light year is the distance travelled by light in one year and is equal to 9,000,000,000,000 kilometres.

The nearest star to our sun, *Proxima Centauri* is over 4 light years away, while some distant stars that we can see are 500 or more light years away. So that, when we are looking at them, what we actually see happened over 500 years ago – before Henry VIII came to the throne!

Our own special star is the Sun. It is special because it is so close to the earth – 150,000,000 kilometres away. Compared to many other stars it is rather small and insignificant, but to us it is very large and vitally important. It provides almost all the heat and light which are needed to support life on earth.

1 Why does the sun seem so large and bright to us compared with other stars? It is much nearer to us

2 Why are distances in the Universe measured in light years? Because distances are so great

3–4 What do all the stars that we can see have in common? They are very hot and bright

5 What would happen to the earth if the sun were to fade? The earth would go cold

[6–17]
The Sun moves through space taking with it a large family of objects, which together are called the **solar system**.

The largest members of the sun's family are called the planets, of which the earth is one. The planets all circle the sun in paths which are called **orbits**.

The orbits of the planets are not strictly circular but are actually ellipses. An ellipse is rather like a squashed circle. **These diagrams cannot be drawn to scale, because the distances between the planets are so large compared with the size of the planets and the sun.**

The time taken for the earth to complete one orbit – to go round the sun exactly once – is one year, which is 365¼ days. So to keep the calendar in step with the earth's orbit we give every fourth year 366 days to allow for this.

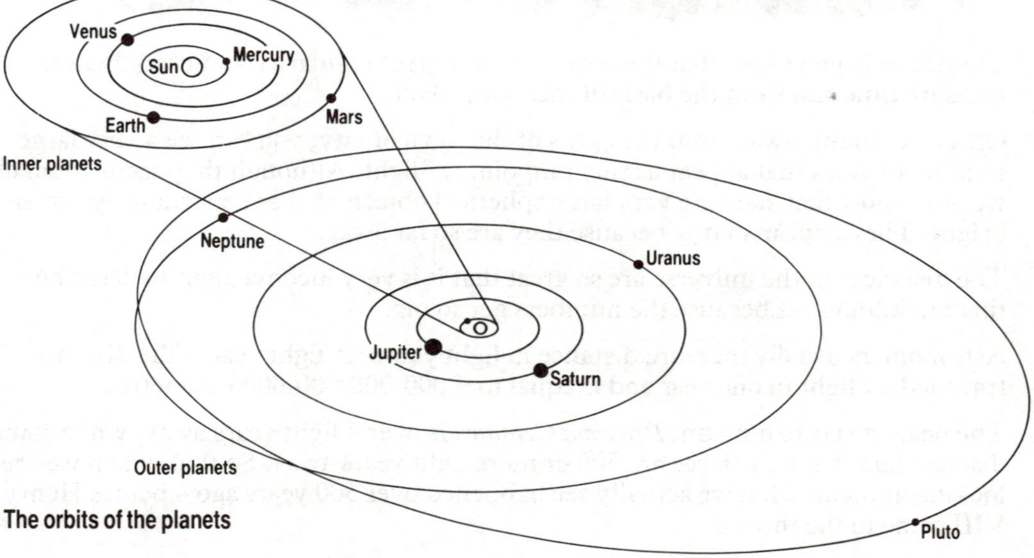

The orbits of the planets

6 When is an extra day added on? At the end of February

7 What is the name given to every fourth year with an extra day? A leap year

As the planets move in their elliptical paths they are also spinning like tops. The earth spins on its axis so that different points on the earth face the sun at different times and give us night and day.

8 How long does it take for the earth to completely revolve on its axis? 24 hours

9 Which of the planets would you expect to have the shortest year (i.e. orbit the sun exactly once)? Mercury

10 Which planet would you expect to have the longest year? Pluto

11 Which of the planets would you expect to be the hottest? Mercury

12 Would you expect it to be as light in daylight on Neptune as it is on earth? No

We get all of our light and warmth from the sun but, in Britain:

13 is the light part of all our days the same length? No

14 how many seasons do we have? 4

15 is it equally warm throughout the year? No

16 does the sun appear equally high in the sky at midday all through the year? No

17 in which month does it appear highest? June

[18–22]
We can explain all these observations by looking carefully at the earth's orbit around the sun.

The earth spins on an imaginary axle or axis passing through the North and South Poles.

If this axis was at right angles to the orbit of the earth all places on the earth would have all their days of equal length – but they do not!

The axis on which the earth spins is tilted at an angle of just over 23° further than the right angle, so that during part of the earth's orbit around the sun the North Pole is in shade all the time and it is dark all day, while at another part of the orbit the North Pole is in sun during the whole 24 hours.

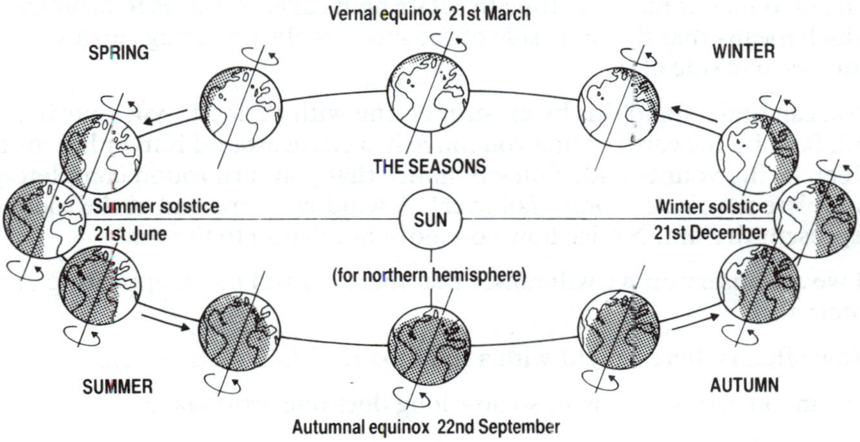

18 The Arctic is often called the 'Land of the Midnight Sun'

19 What do you think happens near the *South* Pole? The same as at the North Pole

20 When? At the opposite time of the year

21 There are two times in the year when the earth's axis *is* at right angles to the earth's orbit. How do you think that this would affect the length of night and day?

They would be equal

We can see that in summer the days are longer and the sun shines more directly overhead, rather than at an angle:

22 Can you see any other reason, from the map of the earth's orbit, why the sun seems hotter and brighter in summer? It is nearer to the earth

The moon

[23–28]
There is another object we often see in the sky and that is the moon. The moon is much closer to the earth than the sun, only 384,400 kilometres compared with the sun, which can be 150,000,000 kilometres away from the earth, nearly 400 times as far.

23 The moon is smaller than any of the planets, yet it appears as one of the largest objects in the sky, nearly as big as the sun. Why is this? It is nearer than the others

24–25 When it shines at night it seems quite bright, although not nearly as bright as the sun. Why is there little warmth in moonlight? The moon is cold Where does the light come from? It is reflected from the sun

The moon takes the same time to rotate on its axis as it does to orbit the earth, which means that the same side of the moon is always facing earth so that we can only see one side of it.

You can understand this by experimenting with a friend. Ask your friend to stand still (and be the earth) while you move in a circle around him or her (as the moon). Keep facing your friend. You will notice that you turn round completely while you complete the circle. (Don't fall over!) A window at one end of the room can represent the sun. Notice how you move in relation to the sun!

If we are observant we will notice that there is a full moon appearing at regular intervals.

26 How often is there a night with a full moon? Every four weeks

27 The moon orbits the earth, so how long does one orbit take? Four weeks

28 What makes the moon shine brightly at night? The sun

[29–33]
An obvious question we might ask is, 'Why does the moon appear in various shapes?' These various shapes are called **phases** of the moon.

29–32 Name the various shapes of the moon in the night sky.

Crescent moon, half moon, gibbous moon or three-quarters moon, full moon

33 Do these shapes appear in a particular order? Yes

[34–39]
How does the moon appear in so many different shapes, or phases, to people viewing it from the earth?

We can best understand this by looking at a drawing.

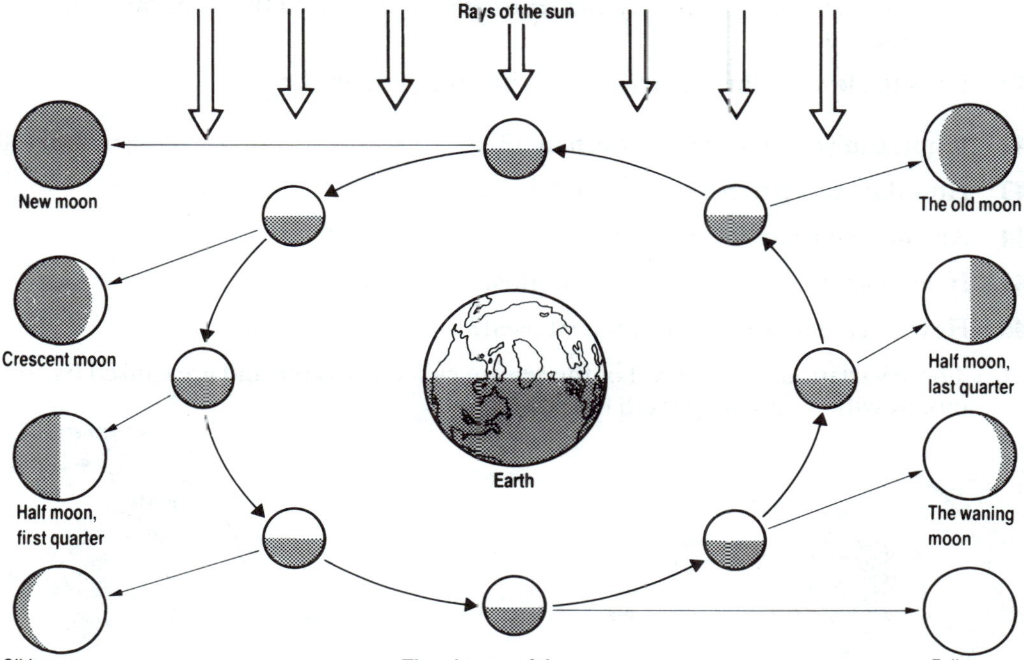

The phases of the moon

The sun's rays only light up the half of the moon which is facing it. Remember the window when you moved round your friend!

34 When the moon is between the sun and the earth we will only see the dark side.

35 When the moon is on the side of the earth furthest from the sun we will see the bright side of the moon.

36 When the moon is at the side of the earth in relation to the sun's rays how much of the illuminated side of the moon will we see? Half

37 Where will the moon be relative to the sun when we see it as a narrow crescent? Near to the sun

During a complete orbit of the moon round the earth:

38 Will a half moon appear more than once? Yes

39 If we see more than one half moon during the cycle and we examine each one with binoculars or a telescope, will we see the same half moon each time? No

The tides

[40–46]
The moon does more for the earth than provide a silvery light to show us our way on dark nights in the countryside. Have you ever noticed the position of the water at the seaside?

40 Does the level of the sea remain the same throughout the day? No

41–42 If not, can you describe a pattern in it? It rises, then falls, rises again, then falls

43 How does this pattern repeat itself daily? High tide comes twice a day

44 Are all high water levels the same? No

45 If not, can you observe a pattern in this? The high tides get higher

46 How often does this pattern repeat itself? Every two weeks

These variations of the level of the sea are called the **tides** and are caused by the moon, with a little help from the sun.

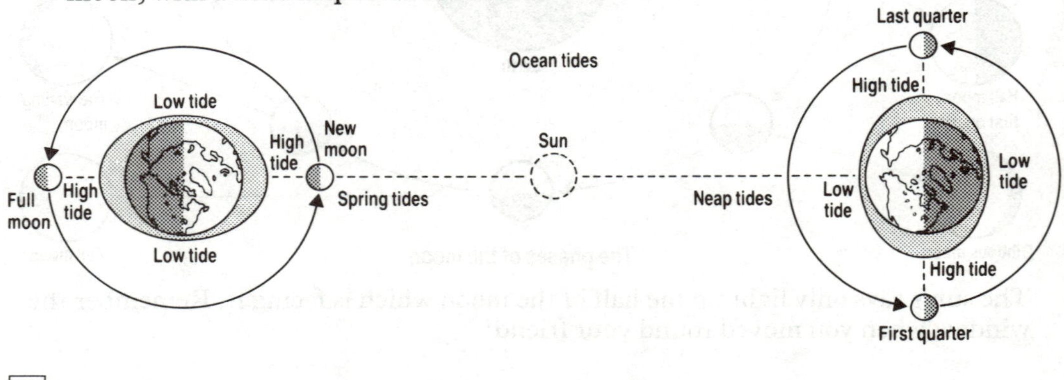

[47–50]

We have all heard of the **force of gravity**. This is a somewhat mysterious force which causes all objects to be attracted towards each other.

The strength of the force between two objects depends on their combined mass (the total amount of matter that each contain) and their distance apart.

A ball falls to earth because the force of gravity is pulling it towards the earth. The force is almost entirely due to the mass of the earth, which is enormous compared to the mass of the ball.

The sun holds the earth and the other planets in orbit around itself because of the gravitational pull between the enormous mass of the sun and the large masses of the planets.

You may understand this better if you imagine swinging a ball on a string in a circle above your head – the string holds the ball in orbit rather like the gravitational force between the sun and the earth or the planets.

The moon is held in orbit around the earth because of the gravitational pull between the moon and the much larger earth.

The gravitational force of the moon and sun attracts the whole earth and everything on it. The moon is much nearer to the earth and so has a greater effect than the sun.

The oceans are liquid and so are free to move.

We can see from the diagram that the moon pulls the oceans of the earth towards itself thus creating high tides on the part of the earth facing the moon. This extra water flows from the rest of the oceans which are at low tide.

There is an equal high point in the balancing oceans on the opposite side of the earth.

As the earth rotates in 24 hours the part of the earth experiencing high tide changes twice.

When the sun and moon are pulling in the same direction the effect is greatest and we have very high and low tides which are called **spring tides**. They occur every 13½ days which is the time taken for the moon to circle half the earth.

47 Which phases of the moon bring very low and very high tides? New moon and full moon

48 Which phases of the moon will have least movement of the tides? Half moons

49–50 Knowing what you now know about the cause of the tides, look back to the diagram in the section **[18–22]**. Can you tell when the highest tides of the year might be expected?

Late September and late March

[51–54]
The earth is warm enough to live on but the moon is very cold – we know this because man has been there! Yet both are equally near to the sun. Which of the following are possible explanations:

51 The earth absorbs more sunlight and reflects less than the moon. (true, false)

52 The earth is kept warm as a result of heat from its molten interior while the moon is cold inside. (true, false)

53 The earth has an atmosphere and this serves as a 'blanket' while the moon does not. (true, false)

54 The earth's relatively fast rotation (24 hours) means that the nights are too short to lose a great deal of heat, while the moon which has very long nights loses most of its heat then. (true, false)

The geology of the earth

How the earth was formed

[55–59]
We believe that the earth was formed from a mass of swirling hot gas over four thousand million years ago. As this mass cooled, the vapours condensed to form rocks and the steam became the water of the oceans.

It is thought that once there was only one enormous mass of land surrounded by oceans. About two hundred million years ago this land mass broke in two and gradually these masses split more and collided to form the mountain ranges and continents we know today.

Over the millions of years which have passed since then, the surface of the earth has changed enormously, and is still changing. Mountains, rivers and deserts have appeared and disappeared.

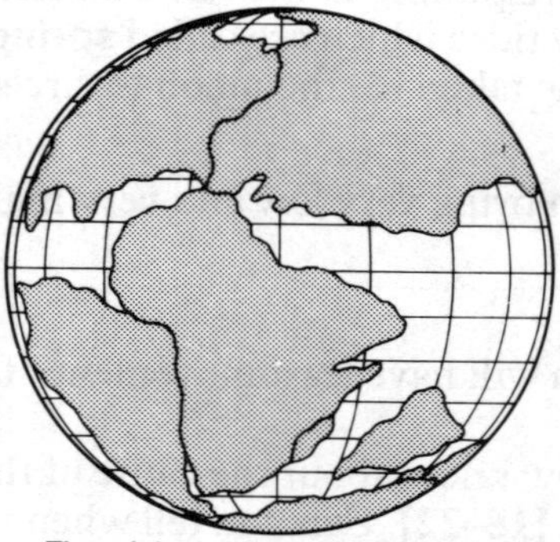

The original shape of the earth's land mass

The shape of the earth's land masses as they look today

Compared with the surface of the earth, little has changed inside. The distance from the surface to the centre of the earth (its radius) is about 6400 kilometres and much of this inside part or **core** still remains very, very hot.

As you can see from the diagram, the core of the earth is about 3500 kilometres thick and consists of an inner solid metallic part, and an outer ring of intensely hot molten material consisting mainly of iron and nickel. The solid centre is equally hot but it is solid because of the tremendous pressures imposed upon it.

Surrounding the core is the **mantle** formed of dense rocks. These are hot enough to be able to flow and change shape, rather like plasticine.

Outside the mantle is the earth's **crust**. This is made of rocks which form the continents and ocean floors. The top layer of the crust is called the **sial** and is composed of solid and comparatively light rocks, like granite.

Underneath the sial and still in the crust is a layer of denser, very hot, rock material called **magma**. This is the material from which the surface rocks that we can see and feel are made.

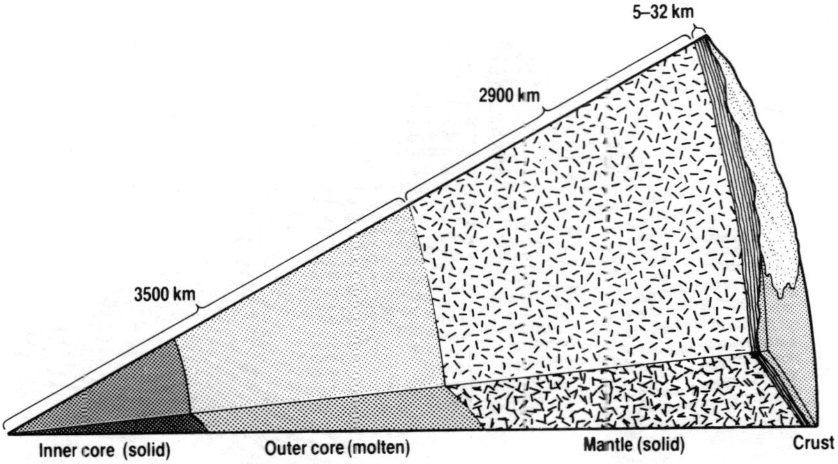

Diagram of a section of the earth

55 Where has most change occurred on the earth over the last 200,000,000 years?

On the surface of the earth

56 Is the core of the earth denser or lighter than the crust? Denser

57 If the core is very, very hot, why is it solid at the centre? Because of the great pressure

58 What did the rocks that we can see at the surface come from? Magma

59 The land masses moved and split into a number of pieces because (they were floating on a liquid or semi-liquid centre, they were floating on the oceans, they were pushed apart by the oceans)

Volcanoes

[60–64]

Fill in the gaps below using these words:

solidified molten volcanic surface magma

Volcanoes occur when the surface of the earth is weak and cracks, releasing the pressure on the hot magma from the lowest part of the earth's crust. When the hot liquid magma breaks through, it streams out of the cracks or fissures as a river of molten rock which is called **lava**. The lava flow contains hot ashes, fragments of rock which have already solidified and steam.

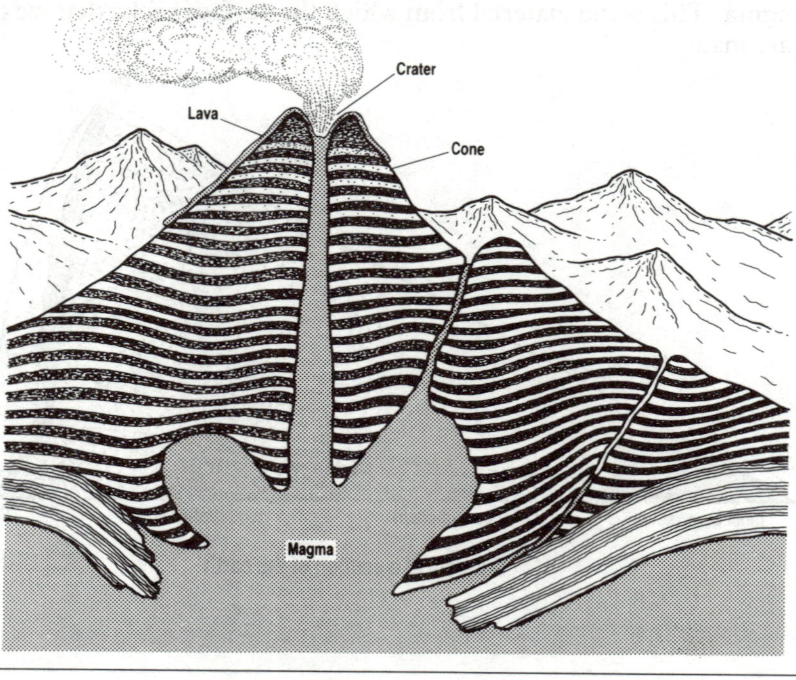

Volcanoes usually occur in the regions where most earthquakes take place, often forming new mountains. One of the most violent volcanic **eruptions** took place on the island of Krakatoa in 1883, the explosive break through of lava producing an enormous tidal wave that affected most of the world's oceans.

Earthquakes

[65–67]
The rocks of the earth's surface are floating on the layer of hot magma which can flow and move. As the core cools down it contracts and the magma moves and flows to take up the space leaving the rigid rocks at the surface pushing against each other.

As millions of years go by this pressure of rocks moving against one other causes them to slide over each other, pile up and form mountains – try pushing the ends of a mat and watch it crease up. The enormous forces involved cause the land to shake and move. The vibrations that are set up are called **shock waves**.

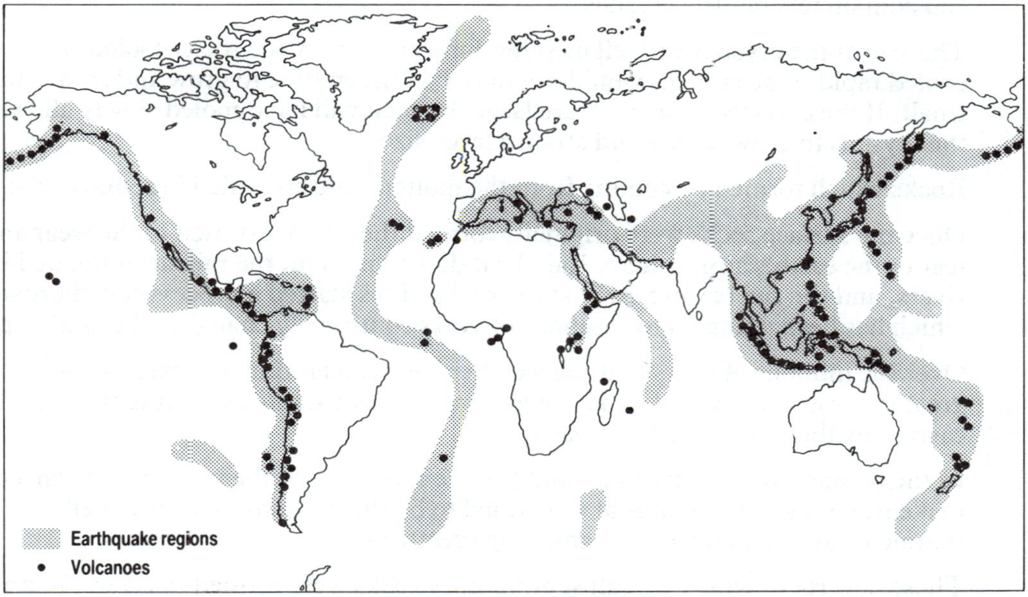

Large mountain ranges are eventually worn down or **eroded** by the weather. Mountains which are still very large have therefore been formed comparatively recently.

Earthquakes are much more common in regions where there are large mountain ranges: on the west coast of North and South America and in eastern Turkey and Armenia.

Earthquakes are much more common in regions where there are large mountain ranges: on the west coast of North and South America and in eastern Turkey and Armenia.

65 Why do earthquakes and volcanoes usually occur in the same regions? They are both caused by the pressure resulting from rocks pushing against each other

66 Why do the rocks of the earth's surface push against each other? Because the core is contracting

67 What are shock waves? They are vibrations caused by the pressures resulting from rocks pushing against each other

Types of rocks

[68–76]
The oldest kinds of rocks that we can usually find are the ones that were made by the original cooling of the earth. Among the oldest rocks we can find in Britain are the **pre-Cambrian** rocks of north-west Scotland and Wales. These are very hard and contain lots of little crystals.

The size of the crystals can tell us something about how the rocks cooled. If they cooled rapidly the crystals would not have had much time to grow and so will be small. If the crystals in the rock are large the rock will have cooled slowly allowing the crystals to grow slowly and attain a large size.

Rocks which formed by cooling from the molten state are called **igneous rocks**.

Once the surface rocks were originally formed they were exposed to the wear and tear of the earth's atmosphere. Rain beat down on them, the rain accumulated into rivers, and the rivers wore away at the rocks. This started a process called **erosion** which has been going on for millions of years continually changing the landscape.

Over the millions of years that the weather has been eroding the earth's surface a great many of the original rocks have been worn down into small fragments and carried by the rivers into the oceans.

In the oceans, the rock particles and fragments settled to the bottom and started to make new rocks. The material was added to by the millions of shells, shell fragments and skeletons of ocean-living creatures.

These new rocks which we call **sedimentary** rocks were formed in layers, like a sandwich, and are quite different from the original igneous rocks.

As new mountains have risen and oceans have changed, many of these sedimentary rocks have emerged from their 'watery grave' to appear at the surface of the earth again.

Often we can find the recognisable remains of shells, animals and plants in sedimentary rocks. These remains, or **fossils**, have been immensely valuable in piecing together the early history of planet Earth and the species which lived on it.

68 If we find fossils in a piece of rock it is likely to be an (igneous, sedimentary) rock. Underline the best answer.

Say whether you think the following statements are **true or false:**

69 Heavy rain will even wear away hard rocks. (true, false)

70 Flowing ice (glaciers) is unlikely to erode rocks. (true, false)

71 Wind blowing dust will erode rocks even in a desert. (true, false)

72 Rocks like slate which show clear signs of layers are igneous rocks. (true, false)

73 The sea erodes the coastline. (true, false)

74 Flat plains are likely to have been much eroded. (true, false)

75 High, jagged mountains are likely to be very old. (true, false)

76 Fossils can tell us much about the history of the rocks containing them. (true, false)

PAPER 3 ATMOSPHERE, CLIMATE AND WEATHER

The earth's atmosphere and how it affects us

[1–3]
The atmosphere is a layer of gases surrounding the earth and extending out into space for about 800 kilometres, though almost all of it lies within 16 kilometres of the earth's surface.

1 What force do you think holds this layer of gases close to the earth and prevents it from escaping into space?

The force of gravity

The main gases in the atmosphere are nitrogen, oxygen and carbon dioxide, as well as water vapour, which often appears as clouds, and a thin layer of a gas called ozone.

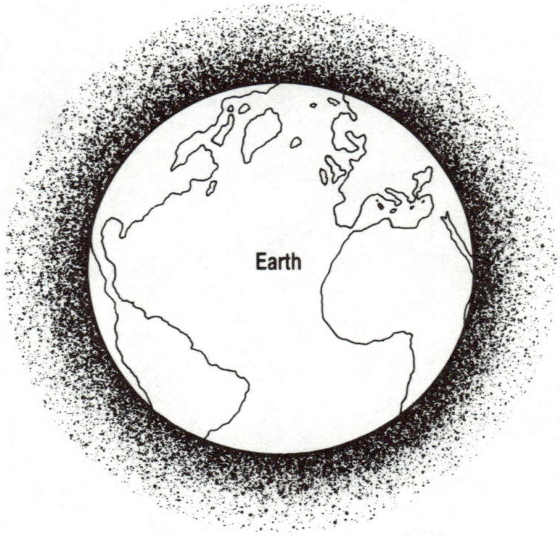

Plants, in sunlight, take in carbon dioxide which they use to make energy-rich chemicals such as sugars, and they give out oxygen.

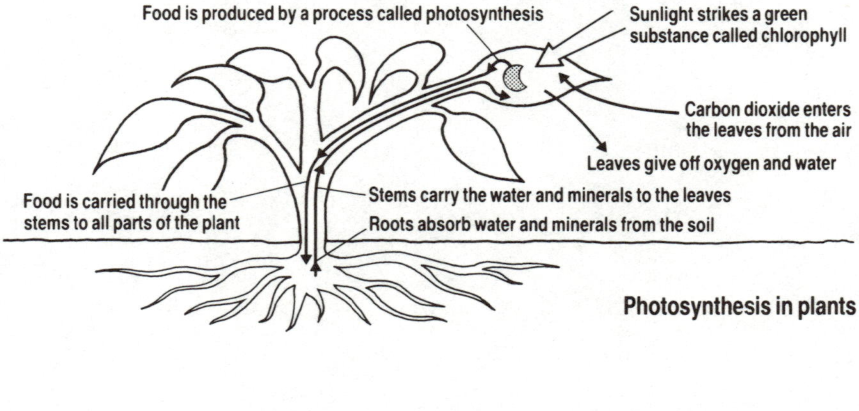

Photosynthesis in plants

2–3 Animals require ....oxygen. to breathe and give out ....carbon dioxide.

[4–10]
Oxygen is the gas that makes things burn. Without oxygen a flame will go out. Fill in the gaps in the paragraphs below using these words:

light rises oxygen candle volume flickers seal

We can find out how much oxygen there is in air with an experiment.

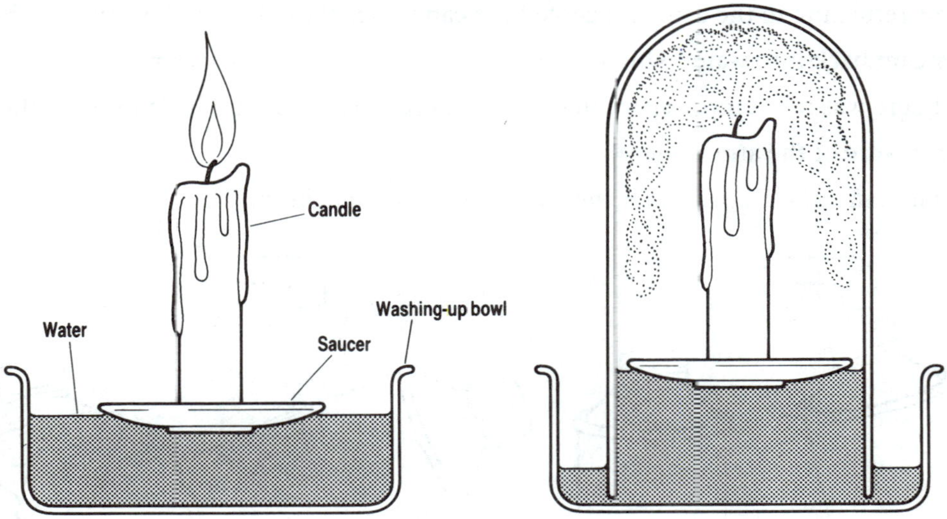

Place a ..candle... on a saucer floating on water in a washing-up bowl.

...Light.. the candle and then put a large glass jar over the candle and saucer until it rests on the bottom of the bowl, the water serving to ...seal.. the jar.

At first the water ....rises. in the jar and then the flame ..flickers.. and goes out.

All the ..oxygen... in the jar has been used and water has risen by about a ⅕ of the ....volume. of the jar, replacing the oxygen.

Atmospheric pressure

[11–20]
Although we think of the gases of the atmosphere as being very light, they weigh a great deal.

The large mass of gas above us in the atmosphere exerts a considerable pressure on all things on the surface of the earth.

11 What is the name of the instrument used to measure this pressure and which helps to predict the weather? ..Barometer...

12–17 Fill in the gaps below using these words:

prevent space collapsed pressure boiled displaced

Scientists demonstrated this ...pressure... by taking a tin can with a screw cap and filling it with a small amount of water.

They heated the can until the water ...boiled... The steam from the boiling water ...displaced... all the air. Then they carefully screwed up the can, to ...prevent... any air returning to the can, and cooled the can under the cold tap. This turned the steam back into water which occupied less ...space... than the steam.

There was now empty space in the can where the air was and little to resist the pressure of the atmosphere.

The can ...collapsed... under the weight of the atmosphere.

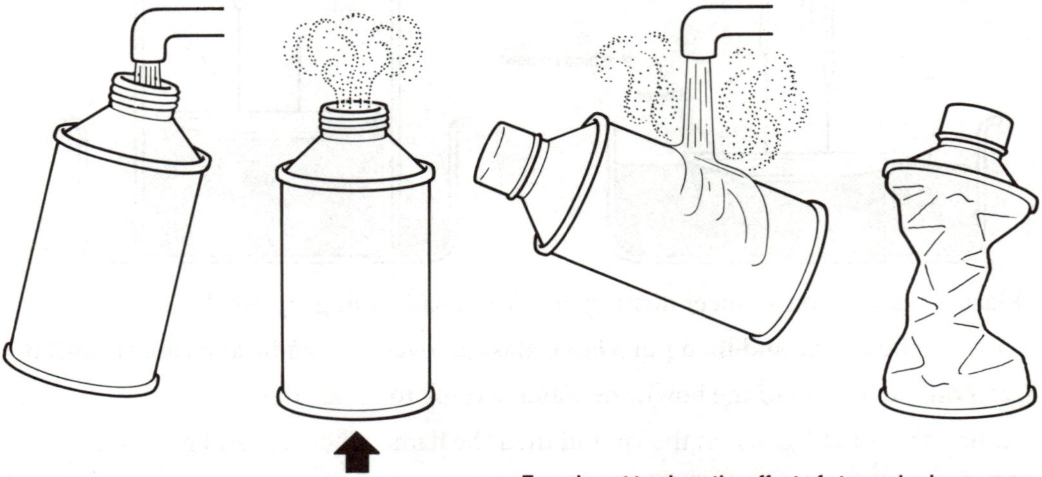

Experiment to show the effect of atmospheric pressure

NOTE – THIS EXPERIMENT IS DANGEROUS AND SHOULD ONLY BE DONE BY A TEACHER. IT SHOULD NOT BE TRIED AT HOME

[18–20]
Underline the best answers:

18 If you climbed to the top of a high mountain, such as Mount Everest would you expect to find the atmospheric pressure (higher, lower)?

19 Would you find it (easier, more difficult) to breathe?

20 Why do long distance runners often come from countries which are very high above sea level? (their lungs are bigger, they are used to making do with less oxygen, they learn to breathe more rapidly)

The atmosphere and climate

[21–25]

The sun's radiation has to pass through the atmosphere before it falls on the earth. The atmosphere controls how much radiation reaches us and how much is retained by the earth.

Most of the sun's radiation is beneficial to life on earth but a small part of it is harmful: this is called **ultraviolet** radiation.

It is normally absorbed by a layer of **ozone**, and so prevented from reaching the surface of the earth.

Ozone is an unusual form of oxygen. Some of it is made from electrical discharges in thunderstorms (in lightning flashes) and some is formed by the sun's radiation. Much of the ozone tends to gather in a layer high in the atmosphere where it shields the earth by absorbing much of the harmful ultraviolet radiation from the sun.

Recently, it has been discovered that some man-made chemicals, for example those used in refrigerators and to pressurise aerosol cans, eventually escape into the upper atmosphere where they encourage the breakdown of this layer of ozone.

The reduction in the ozone layer allows more harmful ultraviolet radiation to reach the earth and it is forecast that, if the ozone layer gets thinner, excessive sunbathing will become increasingly dangerous.

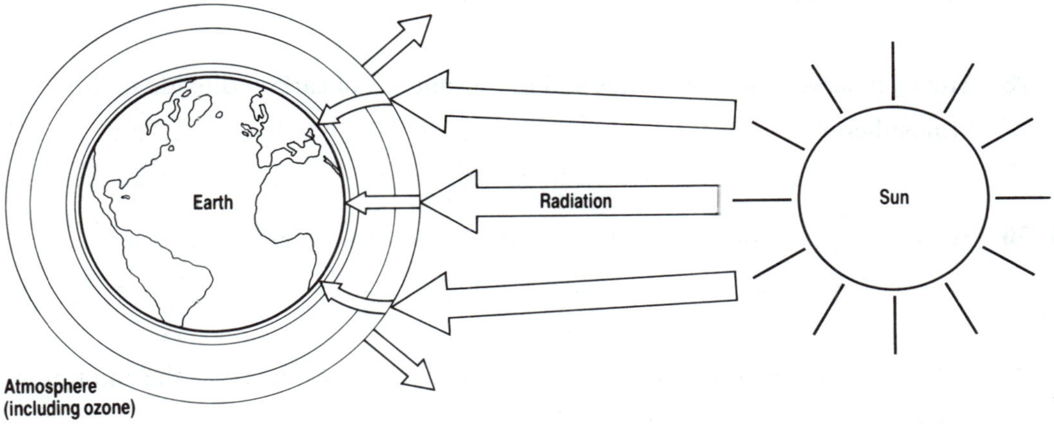

21 Which radiation from the sun is harmful to living things? Ultraviolet radiation

22 What is ozone? An unusual form of oxygen

23–24 What causes ozone to be formed? Radiation from the sun and lightning flashes

25 How can a further loss of the ozone layer be prevented? By reducing the use of the chemicals which cause its breakdown

[26–35]

Another important, although small, part of the atmosphere is carbon dioxide.

Carbon dioxide is made up of molecules of carbon and oxygen and so is produced when all things containing carbon are burnt.

Man and other animals burn food (which contains carbon) to produce energy, and breathe out large amounts of carbon dioxide.

The amount of carbon dioxide in the atmosphere has been kept in balance because plants use carbon dioxide to grow and make more plant substance.

Most inflammable materials such as oil, coal and gas contain carbon and when these are burnt by power stations, cars and domestic heating, vast amounts of carbon dioxide are produced.

In recent years carbon dioxide production from these sources has been increasing enormously, faster than plants can use it, and the amount of carbon dioxide in the atmosphere is increasing.

It is forecast that this increase in carbon dioxide in the atmosphere will cause something called the 'Greenhouse Effect'.

26 For many thousands of years the amount of carbon dioxide in the atmosphere remained the same. Why?

It was kept in balance because animals produced it and plants used it

27 Why has the amount of atmospheric carbon dioxide suddenly started to increase over the last 100 years? Because we use large amounts of energy and burn oil, coal and gas

28 How will large scale forest fires add to the amount of carbon dioxide in the atmosphere? Burning trees will increase the amount of carbon dioxide available, and there will be fewer trees to use it up

29–30 Why can't plants on earth keep up with the increase in carbon dioxide? Because of the huge increase in its production and because there are less plants to use it as a result of the loss of many tropical rainforests

31 Why will cutting down large areas of tropical rain forest increase the amount of carbon dioxide in the atmosphere? Because they consume large amounts of carbon dioxide

32 Why are these areas being cleared? To make more room for people and to grow food

33 How do you suggest that the rise in carbon dioxide might be reduced?

By burning less oil, coal and gas, using energy more efficiently, and by preserving as much plant material as possible

34 Why do plants use carbon dioxide? To make more plant material.

35 When we say that until 100 years ago carbon dioxide was in balance what do we mean? It stayed at a constant amount or carbon dioxide production did not exceed the ability of plants to use it

The Greenhouse Effect

[36–50]
Have you ever stood in a greenhouse on a warm sunny day and noticed that it was much hotter in the greenhouse than it was outside?

There is a very good reason for this.

The radiation from the sun contains light of many colours from ultraviolet light (which the eye cannot see) through to violet, blue, green, yellow and red which are all visible to the human eye.

This is called a **spectrum** and beyond red light the radiation continues, although we cannot see it, into the infra-red.

This invisible infra-red light, which is nearest to visible red light in the spectrum, is radiant heat – it feels warm.

This infra-red light and heat passes through glass, and warms the soil and interior structure of a greenhouse. You can prove this! Hold your hand near to an electric lamp – it feels warm. Place a piece of glass between the lamp and your hand – it still feels warm. The radiated heat from the lamp has passed through the glass.

The warmed soil and interior structure of the greenhouse will radiate heat by themselves. The heat that they radiate is further from visible red than infra-red light and this radiation will not pass through glass. Again you can prove this for yourself! Hold your hand near to the side of a hot radiator – it feels warm. Now place a piece of glass between your hand and the radiator – you no longer feel the warmth. The glass will not allow this radiation to pass.

In this way much of the sun's heat becomes trapped in the greenhouse.

The layer of carbon dioxide in the atmosphere acts very much like the glass in a greenhouse. It allows much of the sun's radiant heat to reach the surface of the earth but will not allow the heat energy which is radiated back by the earth to escape, and so the earth gets warmer.

In the same way, curtains or venetian blinds which are drawn in a sunny room *do not* prevent the room getting too hot. The window glass still allows the heat in but prevents the heat radiated back by the curtains or blinds from getting out.

Shutters on the outside of the glass *do* keep the room cool by preventing the sun's rays getting into the room at all. This is why external shutters are so popular in warm countries.

36 Can the eye see all the sun's radiation? No

37 Which colour is the warmest? Red

38 What does glass do in a greenhouse? It traps the heat

39 What will the 'greenhouse effect' do to the temperature of the earth? Cause it to warm up

40–42 Can you suggest what some consequences of this might be?

Melting of polar ice

The rise in the level of the seas

The more rapid growth of plants

43 Do you think that these consequences will be good for the planet? Probably not

44 Might one effect be to increase the growth of plants? Yes

45 Why do you think this? Plants grow faster when it is warmer

46 Do you think a new satisfactory balance might arise? Possibly

47–50 Describe some of the ways in which you think that a new balance might, or might not, come about.

The increased plant growth will use up more carbon dioxide

The warmer climate would mean we would use less energy for heating

The increased warmth and higher sea level might lead to an increase in rainfall

An increase in rainfall might make the deserts more fertile and provide more space for plant growth

Climate and weather

Temperature

[51–56]
Climate is the average type of weather occurring in a place over a number of years. We can say that Britain has a cool, rather wet **climate**, although sometimes it may be sweltering in a heat wave.
To remark about the heat wave is to talk about the **weather**.

The **climate** of a place depends mainly on the intensity of the sunshine it receives. The power of the sun is at its greatest when it is directly overhead and becomes much less powerful the lower it is in the sky.

Consequently, places with a hot climate are near to the equator and those with a cold climate are near to the poles.

The earth may be roughly divided into three areas with the same sort of climate.

Near the North and South poles are the **polar regions** which get the weakest sunlight. These are very cold and have snow and ice all the year round, although there are very big differences between summer and winter.

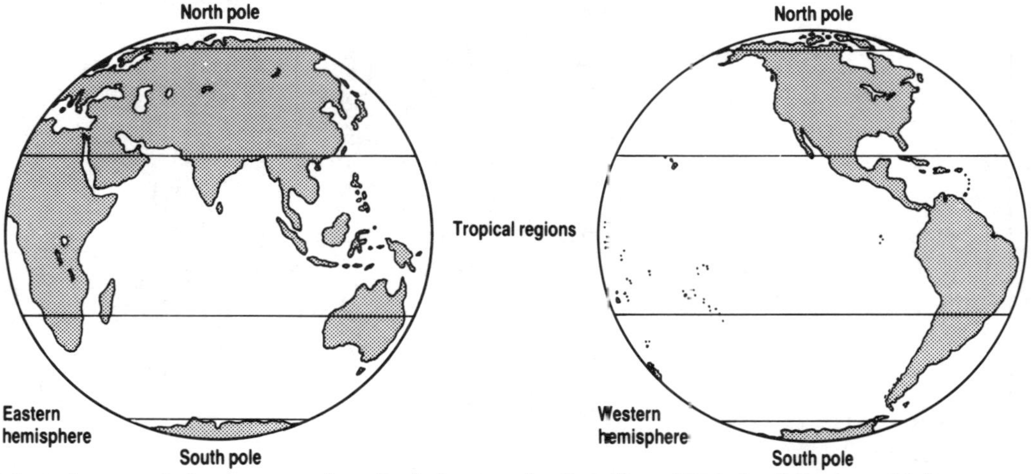

A band around the equator is called the **tropical region**. This is the area which gets the strongest sunlight and is hot all the year round, with very little **seasonal** difference.

The broad belt in between the polar region and the tropics is called the **temperate region**. Here the temperatures do not get excessively hot or cold. There are fairly large differences between summer and winter.

Climate is also affected by the sea. The oceans gain heat from the sun more slowly than from the land, and hold it for very much longer.

The land warms up quickly under the hot sun. It can get much warmer than the sea and if it is near to a cool sea it is prevented from getting very hot by the cool sea breezes.

Similarly, on cold days the land loses heat relatively quickly. It can become cooler than the surrounding sea, which prevents it from becoming excessively cold.

Because of this, islands usually have a **temperate climate** with relatively small fluctuations of temperature, while places far inland tend to have an extreme climate with very large changes in the temperature between day and night and summer and winter.

The height of a place above sea level also influences climate. High areas tend to be much colder than low-lying places.

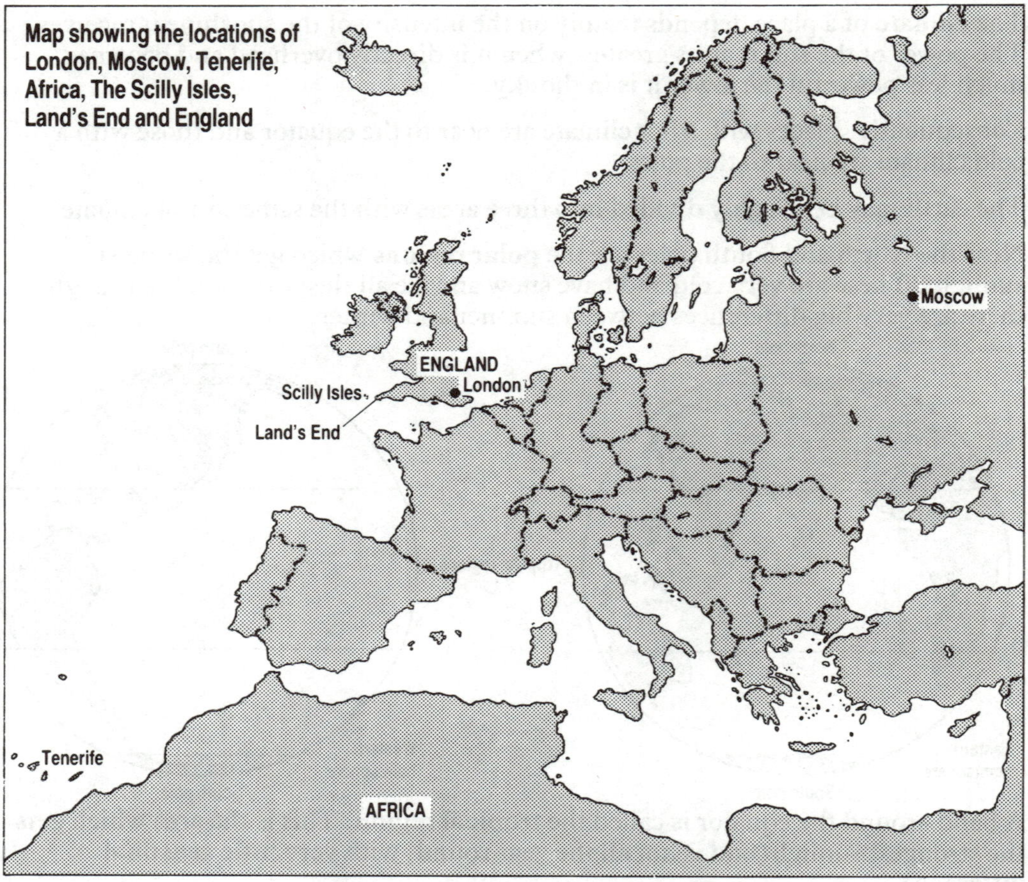

51–52 London and Moscow are equally north of the equator. Would you expect their climates to be similar? No Why or why not? London is near to the sea Moscow is far inland

53–54 Tenerife is a mountainous island off the coast of Africa and fairly close to the tropics. Would you expect the climate to be the same all over the island? .... Why, or why not? The mountains would be much cooler than the coastal areas and produce more rain

55–56 The Scilly Isles are small islands lying off Land's End which is at the southwest tip of England. Give two reasons why the Scilly Isles might have the most temperate climate in Britain. They are at the southern end of Britain and are small islands surrounded by fairly warm sea

Rainfall

[57–62]
Fill in the gaps in the paragraphs below using words from this list:

clouds wind water rain energy moist

Another important feature of climate is rainfall.

The sun's ...energy... warms the oceans and lakes causing some of the ...water... to **evaporate** making the air moist. This warm ...moist... air rises and as it cools, the water **condenses** to form ...clouds... just like the steam from a boiling kettle. The clouds are **dispersed**, or driven far and wide by the ...wind... until they encounter cold air. When the air cools more the water falls as ...rain...

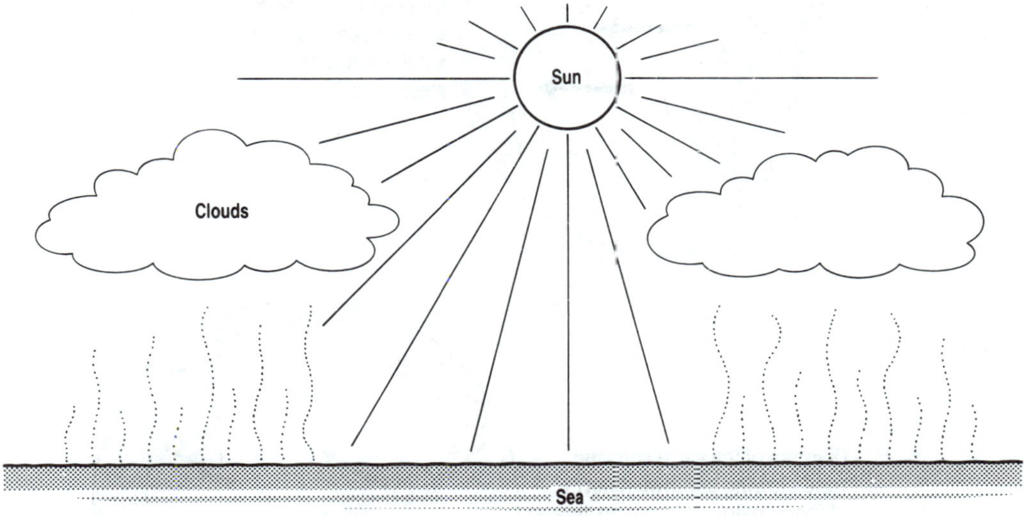

Winds

[63–66]
As the earth rotates on its axis it drags its atmosphere with it and there is continuous slippage between the atmosphere and the surface of the earth.

This will appear to us on earth as a wind blowing from west to east. This is why the commonest wind direction we experience is from the west.

Because the sun is strongest near the equator, the land and sea are warmer there. This means that the air is warmer. The warm air rises and spreads out tending to push some of the atmosphere to the north and south. These are the main causes of the winds.

Watch several streams of water flowing into a pool, you will notice that they make lots of whirlpools and eddies and the faster the flow the more whirling and eddying there is.

Exactly the same thing happens when two major air flows mix, and so the world's winds are much more complicated then we suggested before.

It is these variations which produce the **weather** which changes from day to day.

63 The rotation of the earth tends to cause winds to blow from the ..west...

64 What happens as two different air flows meet? ..They form whirlpools and eddies..

65 What makes the air warm near to the equator? ..The heat of the sun..

66 What happens to this air? ..It rises and spreads out..

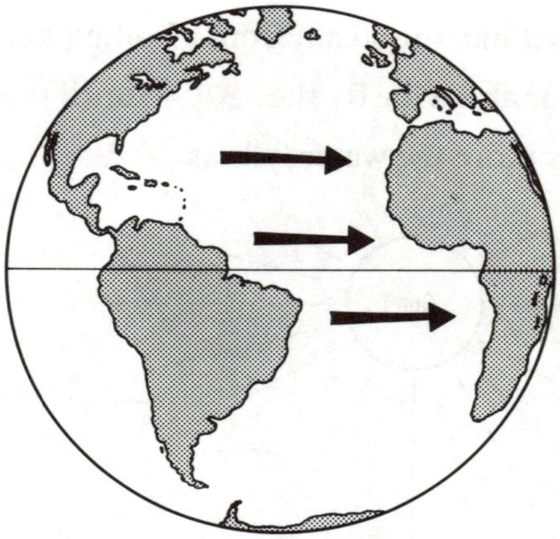

Diagram of the earth with arrows showing wind blowing from west to east

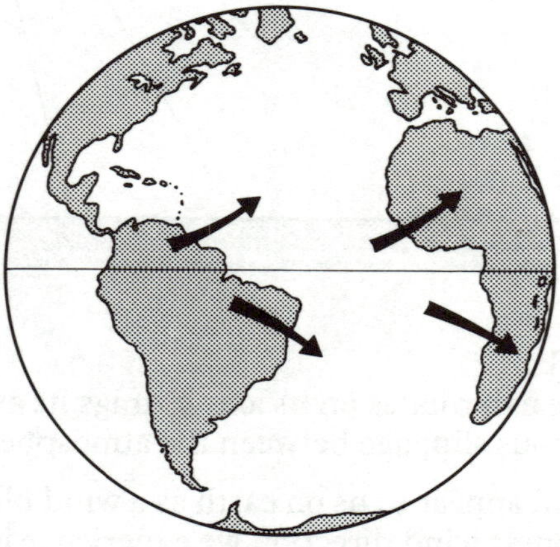

Diagram of the earth showing wind blowing southwest north of the Equator and from northwest south of the Equator

What makes it rain?

[67–70]

Warm air holds much more water vapour than cold air so that if warm moist air is cooled, water condenses. Hold a cold glass mirror near to the spout of a steaming kettle and notice the water droplets form.

TAKE CARE THAT YOU DON'T BURN YOURSELF ON THE HOT STEAM!

If moist, warm air encounters much cooler air it will first form clouds and if the air is cooled enough it will rain.

Air is normally much colder higher up than it is near to the ground, so that conditions which force warm, moist air to rise will produce cloud and rain.

In this picture the wind is blowing over the sea:

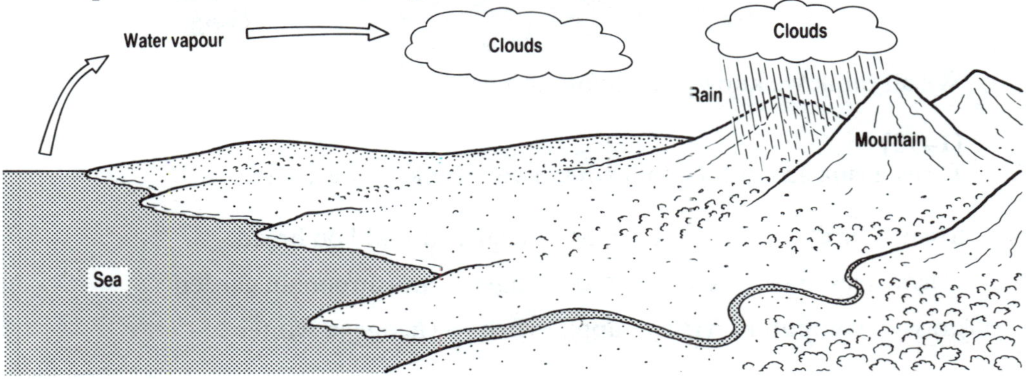

67 Will the air be moist or dry? Moist

68 What forces the air to rise? The mountains

69 Why will it rain on the windward side of the mountain? Because it is there that the moist air will be cooled forming clouds and rain

70 Why will the land on the other side of the mountain have less rain than the land facing the wind? The air will have lost much of its moisture and warmed up again as it drops down after passing the mountain

Britain gets so much cloud and rain because the wind most frequently comes from the west or southwest after passing over many kilometres of the Atlantic Ocean and is very moist.

When the wind comes to Britain from the east it has been passing over many kilometres of the dry land of continental Europe and contains much less moisture. Usually east winds bring dry weather.

71 The westerly wind which is more common gives Britain its cloudy, rainy climate

72 The occasional easterly winds bring spells of dry weather

PAPER 4 THE VARIETY OF LIFE

Exploring living things

There is an enormous variety of living things all around us. Other human beings, dogs, cats, birds, spiders, bees and wasps are just a few of the species (the kinds of animals) we encounter every day.
Within these species there are considerable differences. From Great Danes to little Yorkshire Terriers, dogs show a great variety of size, colour and shape.

We all think we know what living things are, but do we?

[1–13]
Draw a ring around the following if you think they are alive.

fossil	bird	robot	seed	lizard	mould on bread
worm	rosebush	crab	nest	tiger	mushroom in garden
grass	computer	virus	apple	fish	hedge in winter

[14–24]
To be able to study, describe or even talk about living things we need to divide them up into different types – to **classify them**.

The easiest and clearest division we can make is between **plants** and **animals.**

Differences between plants and animals

Plants get their food from the simple substances which they absorb from the air or the soil. They build up the complicated materials they need for growth from these simple substances using the energy obtained from sunlight.

Green plants contain **chlorophyll** which is a green pigment with the unique ability to collect and use energy from the sun. This enables the plant to use the sun's energy to make the chemicals it needs both for nourishment and growth.

Animals get their food by eating plants or other animals, using the relatively complicated chemicals already made by the plants or other animals, to provide fuel and building materials for their own bodies.

A scientist might ask, 'What are some of the most important differences between animals and plants?'

Use words from this list to fill in the gaps below:

seeds limbs roots skeleton salts move skeletons leaves food muscles plants animals

14 Plants do not move from place to place but are normally anchored to the ground by their ...roots... which they also use to absorb water and nutrients.

15 They breathe air and absorb energy from sunlight through their ...leaves...

16 Most plants reproduce by making ...seeds...

17 They have no internal or external ...skeletons... but support themselves by the stiffness of their cell walls which are made of a 'woody' substance called **cellulose**.

18 Their roots can grow over great distances in the search for water and ...salts..., but essentially they never move as a single unit.

19–21 Many animals have a ...skeleton... and usually ...move... around to obtain ...food...

22–23 They are most often specially equipped for movement and possess ...muscles... to operate their ...limbs...

24 ...Animals... react to stimuli almost instantaneously; when ...plants... react to stimuli, such as strong sunlight, they need to be stimulated for longer, and they react over a long period of time.

[25–27]
Plants can be divided into ones which produce flowers and seeds – flowering plants; and ones which do not produce flowers and seeds – non-flowering plants. Some flowers are very tiny; some are hard to see because they are green.

Underline the non-flowering plants:

roses	geraniums	<u>ferns</u>	apple trees	grasses	<u>mushrooms</u>
pansies	<u>pinetrees</u>	chestnuts	holly	buttercups	

A variety of animals

[28–36]
We can divide animals into those with their skeletons inside their flesh and with a spine or vertebra – which we call **vertebrates**; and those with a skeleton outside their body in the form of a shell, or lacking any skeleton at all – which are called **invertebrates**.

Underline the invertebrates in this list:

horse	frog	<u>snail</u>	snake	<u>bee</u>	bat	starling	<u>slug</u>	cat	mouse
<u>worm</u>	<u>crab</u>	trout	<u>octopus</u>	duck	ape	<u>starfish</u>	<u>beetle</u>	<u>ant</u>	lizard

[37–40]
The invertebrate animals can be further divided into no less than nine groups depending on their physical characteristics: for example, the **crustaceans** such as crabs, lobsters, prawns and shrimps all have an external shell and almost all live in water.

The huge group of **insects** all possess six legs and, usually wings; examples are butterflies, ants, bees and beetles, while the spiders, scorpions, ticks and mites have eight walking legs and are all called the **arachnids**.

What class of invertebrates do these pictures show?

37 crustacean

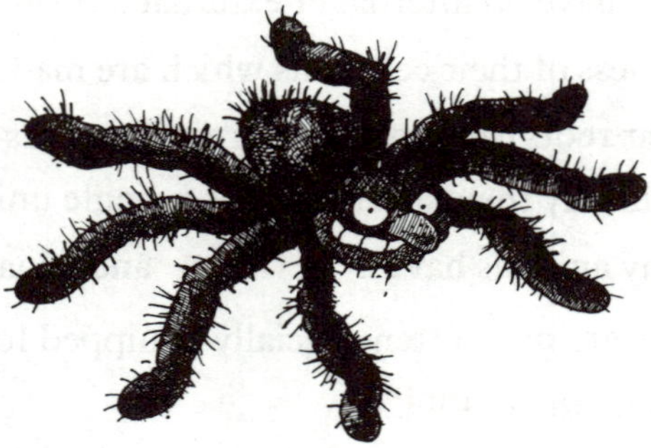

38 arachnid

39 insect

40 insect

[41–44]
Some vertebrates keep their body temperature constant and usually at a higher temperature than their environment. They are called **warm-blooded**.

In others, the body temperature varies with the temperature of the environment in which the animal finds itself. We call these animals **cold-blooded**.

Draw a ring around each cold-blooded animal in this list:

herring duck penguin frog tortoise crocodile

seal cow whale ape man polar bear

The cold blooded vertebrates can be divided into three groups:

Fish which live exclusively in water. They breathe by gills which extract oxygen from the water and are covered with scales.

Amphibia have no scales on their bodies and live both in water and on land, this group includes newts, toads and frogs.

Reptiles are animals with scaly bodies and include snakes and lizards. Almost all live on land.

The warm-blooded animals are the birds and mammals. They keep their bodies at a warm and constant temperature compared to their environment.

The processes on which the animal depends: digestion, respiration and muscular activity proceed faster at temperatures between 35 and 45°C, which is often considerably warmer than their environment. Because they stay warm, they can live and move around in different conditions.

They keep warm when it is cold by using more food and keep cool when it is excessively hot by sweating and losing heat by evaporation.

[45–49]
Can you suggest how these animals conserve their body heat?

45 Rabbit It is covered by a thick layer of fur

46 Pig It has a thick layer of fat under its skin

47 Sheep Are covered with wool

48 Whale It has a thick layer of fat (blubber) under its skin

49 Humans Wear clothes

[50–53]
How might a warm-blooded animal such as a mouse and a cold-blooded animal such as a frog behave under different conditions?

Cross out the unwanted word:

50–51 In a warm room the frog is (active, ~~inactive~~) the mouse is (active, ~~inactive~~).

52–53 In a very cold room the frog is (~~active~~, inactive) and the mouse is (active, ~~inactive~~).

Variation and adaptation

[54–57]
There is great variation even among similar kinds of animals and plants. Among human beings we are all more suited to some tasks than others.

For example, successful long-distance runners are normally of a quite different physical type from discus or javelin throwers or weight lifters.

It is easier to run fast and far if you are slender with long legs, have a relatively slow pulse-rate, large lungs and the ability not to tire easily.

For weightlifting on the other hand, it helps to be very 'beefy' with a great deal of muscle power in the arms, shoulders and legs. The need is to produce a 'thrust' or 'throw' of a heavy weight for a very short time.

54–55 What sport would you suggest that a tall, light girl with very long legs might be good at? Sprinting and jumping

56–57 What do you think are two of the most important physical features of a racing greyhound? A light, streamlined body and long, slender legs

[58–63]
Among the birds we can see a considerable variety of wing shapes which are adapted to its lifestyle.

The seagull has long, relatively narrow, wings which enable it to glide and soar on air currents, remaining aloft for long periods of time. It can make long sea crossings with very little effort.

The owl has broad wings which it flaps only slowly giving almost silent flight suited to stealthy hunting at night.

The cold blooded vertebrates can be divided into three groups:

Fish which live exclusively in water. They breathe by gills which extract oxygen from the water and are covered with scales.

Amphibia have no scales on their bodies and live both in water and on land, this group includes newts, toads and frogs.

Reptiles are animals with scaly bodies and include snakes and lizards. Almost all live on land.

The warm-blooded animals are the birds and mammals. They keep their bodies at a warm and constant temperature compared to their environment.

The processes on which the animal depends: digestion, respiration and muscular activity proceed faster at temperatures between 35 and 45°C, which is often considerably warmer than their environment. Because they stay warm, they can live and move around in different conditions.

They keep warm when it is cold by using more food and keep cool when it is excessively hot by sweating and losing heat by evaporation.

[45–49]
Can you suggest how these animals conserve their body heat?

45 Rabbit It is covered by a thick layer of fur

46 Pig It has a thick layer of fat under its skin

47 Sheep Are covered with wool

48 Whale It has a thick layer of fat (blubber) under its skin

49 Humans Wear clothes

[50–53]
How might a warm-blooded animal such as a mouse and a cold-blooded animal such as a frog behave under different conditions?

Cross out the unwanted word:

50–51 In a warm room the frog is (active, ~~inactive~~) the mouse is (active, ~~inactive~~).

52–53 In a very cold room the frog is (~~active~~, inactive) and the mouse is (active, ~~inactive~~).

Variation and adaptation

[54–57]
There is great variation even among similar kinds of animals and plants. Among human beings we are all more suited to some tasks than others.

For example, successful long-distance runners are normally of a quite different physical type from discus or javelin throwers or weight lifters.

It is easier to run fast and far if you are slender with long legs, have a relatively slow pulse-rate, large lungs and the ability not to tire easily.

For weightlifting on the other hand, it helps to be very 'beefy' with a great deal of muscle power in the arms, shoulders and legs. The need is to produce a 'thrust' or 'throw' of a heavy weight for a very short time.

54–55 What sport would you suggest that a tall, light girl with very long legs might be good at? Sprinting and jumping

56–57 What do you think are two of the most important physical features of a racing greyhound? A light, streamlined body and long, slender legs

[58–63]
Among the birds we can see a considerable variety of wing shapes which are adapted to its lifestyle.

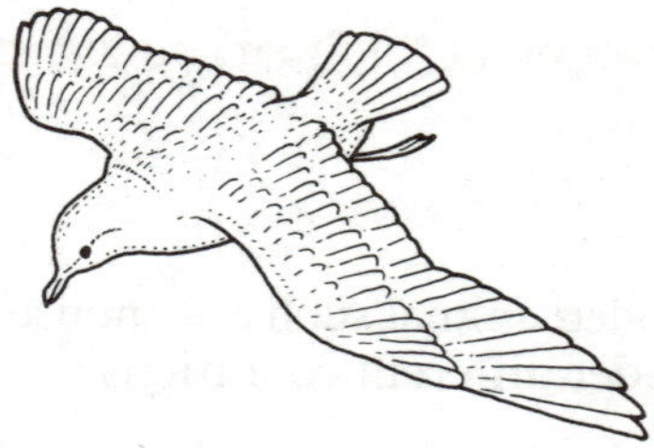

The seagull has long, relatively narrow, wings which enable it to glide and soar on air currents, remaining aloft for long periods of time. It can make long sea crossings with very little effort.

The owl has broad wings which it flaps only slowly giving almost silent flight suited to stealthy hunting at night.

The sparrow has broad, short wings which it flaps rapidly to give a short, rapid take off from the ground or tree. This is good for tree hopping and short distances, but not suitable for long sustained flight.

Can you think of some other adaptations which suit birds for the way they live, the food that they eat or the way they catch their food?

58 What does the long neck of the swan or heron enable them to do?

Dip their heads deep underwater for fish

59 A pelican has a large beak which enables it to carry large amounts of fish.

60 Why are a flamingo's very long neck and legs useful and necessary?

For fishing and wading in lakes and ponds

61 A racehorse's body is adapted for running fast

62 A cat is ideally suited for short bursts of speed which enable it to

hunt and catch its prey

63 A giraffe's long legs and very long neck allow it to graze on the leaves of trees which other animals cannot reach

[64–66]

The **environment** often has a strong effect on the varieties of species in it.

In the arctic region bears, foxes, rabbits and other animals are often white or silvery grey, so they will blend into their surroundings and escape detection by hunters or by their prey.

A brown bear in the arctic snow would be an easy target for his enemies; a polar bear in the green forests of the American West would be an easier target than a black or brown one.

Underline the best answer in the brackets:

64 Where would you expect to find brilliantly coloured birds? (polar regions, very high mountains, flower-filled jungles)

65 The fact that so many polar animals are white probably shows that (the cold turns their fur white, white or lighter animals are more likely to live longer and have offspring like themselves, white fur is warmer, living in the north makes them age more quickly).

66 The facility arctic animals have for blending into their surroundings is a way of (disguising, camouflaging, eliminating, damaging) themselves.

The **environment** also has a profound effect on the species of plants that grow in it.

Dry, arid regions only support those plants which can conserve water.

Many species of cactii live in desert regions and are specially adapted to retain water, to collect dew and to store water in cells with virtually watertight skins. They flower very rapidly after a rainstorm in order to produce seeds quickly in the short time when conditions are favourable.

Where it is cold, with only short summers and long, icy and dark winters we find plants which can mature rapidly, produce flowers and seed in the brief summer so that the seed is scattered and ready to germinate and yield new plants in the following year.

[67–76]
Fill in the blanks or underline the correct answer in the brackets:

67 In Britain, we live in a climate where there are 4...... seasons. We plant in the spring, grow things in the summer, harvest in the autumn and have our coldest weather in the winter.

68–69 In some parts of the world, there are only 2...... recognisable seasons: wet and dry......

70 One of the great problems in these areas is when rainfall is inadequate. We call this time a drought......

Many plants have a life-cycle adapted to the two-season year. They can be planted in the dry season, will grow in the very wet season, and can be harvested when the period of rapid watering and growth has finished.

71–72 These plants are used to having plenty of water in the rainy season, and die without it. If a country has not received enough rainfall for several years, one solution for its crops might be to select plants which could learn to grow with less water...... and yet tolerate the larger...... amount.

73 This would make them (stronger, greener, more adaptable, tastier).

74 Another solution to the same problem would be for the plant to be able to (manufacture, store, dig for, collect) water.

75–76 One famous group of plants which do this are cacti...... which often live in desert...... regions, but unfortunately they are not a useful food crop because animals cannot eat them.

Energy makes things happen!

To most of us energy is a mysterious term. We often cannot see, touch or hear energy we can only experience its effects. We can tell that the rays of the sun have energy because they provide light and keep us warm (light and heat energy). We know gunpowder has energy, because it will explode, causing damage and making noise (sound energy), and we can tell that a moving car has energy because if it hits a wall it will cause destruction. We can only describe energy by the effects it has on other things. Energy is the ability to do work.

[1–4]
Are these people using energy?

1

Yes

2

Yes

3

Yes

4

No

We can describe energy according to the way it produces results. We can say we have used **mechanical energy** to lift a book onto a shelf or to throw a brick through a window. **Sound energy** is a kind of mechanical energy, caused by making the air vibrate. If we drop a heavy object, there is a bang.

Chemical energy is the energy stored in materials which is released when there is a chemical reaction, for example, if the material is burned. Here the energy is changed to **heat**, and often to **light** as well.

[5–10]

5 Does the football have much energy in the first picture? No

6 Does the ball have more energy in the second picture? Yes

7 What kind of energy does the ball have now? Mechanical energy

8 Where does it get its energy from? The girl kicking it

9 What happens to the energy of the ball in the third picture?
It gives some of it to the window

10 Some of the energy is changed to sound

[11–20]

11 Does it require more energy to lift a book from the floor to a table than a pencil?
Yes

12–15 When you light a firework such as a rocket, energy is produced by burning chemicals. Which forms of energy are produced? Heat and light and sound and mechanical

16 How does a cow get the energy to produce milk? By eating grass

17 Where does grass get the energy to grow? From the sun

8–20 If you inflate a balloon, what form of energy do you put into the balloon?

Mechanical

What kinds of energy are produced when you let it go, without sealing off the neck?

Sound and Mechanical

[21–23]

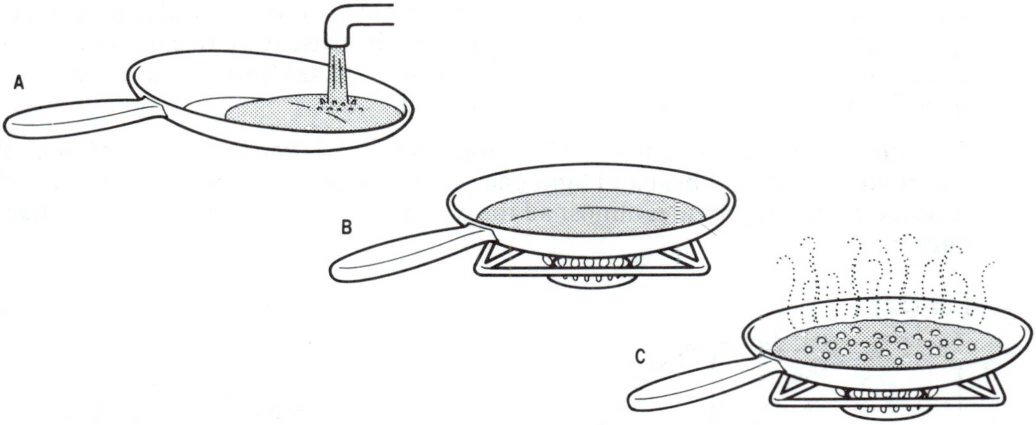

21 In which pan does the water have most energy? C

22 Where does it get its energy from? The heat of the burning gas

23 What sorts of energy can you recognise in B and C? Heat, light and sound

4–27 Which forms of energy can you identify here? Heat and sound and light and mechanical

How energy changes

Electrical energy can be produced from chemical energy in a battery, or from mechanical energy in a power station. We know it is there because we can use it to drive an electric motor, which will produce mechanical energy, or light a lamp, which converts the energy into light and heat.

Nuclear energy is the energy locked up in the atoms of matter and is released by splitting the atom. We know the energy is there because if we release it in a controlled way an enormous amount of heat is produced from which large quantities of electrical energy can be generated.

The Sun is a vast swirling mass of burning gas which is very, very hot, giving off enormous amounts of heat and light energy. The small amount of this energy which reaches the Earth provides almost all the energy of the earth and we call it **solar energy**.

[28–30]

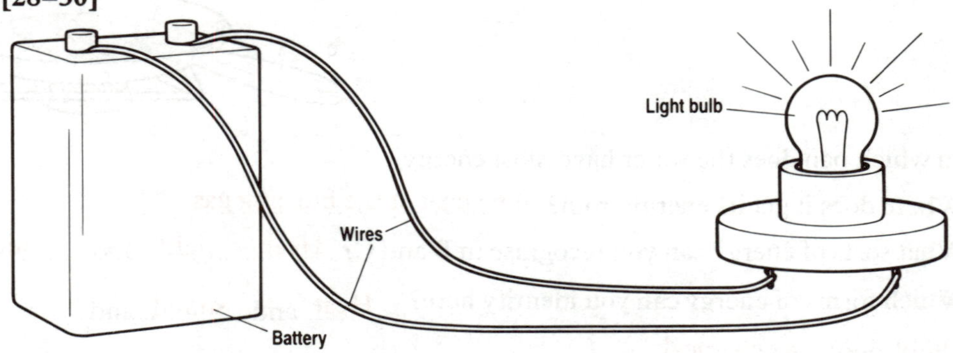

28–29 This picture shows that chemical energy can change into light energy.

30 What other kind of energy would you expect to be produced? Heat

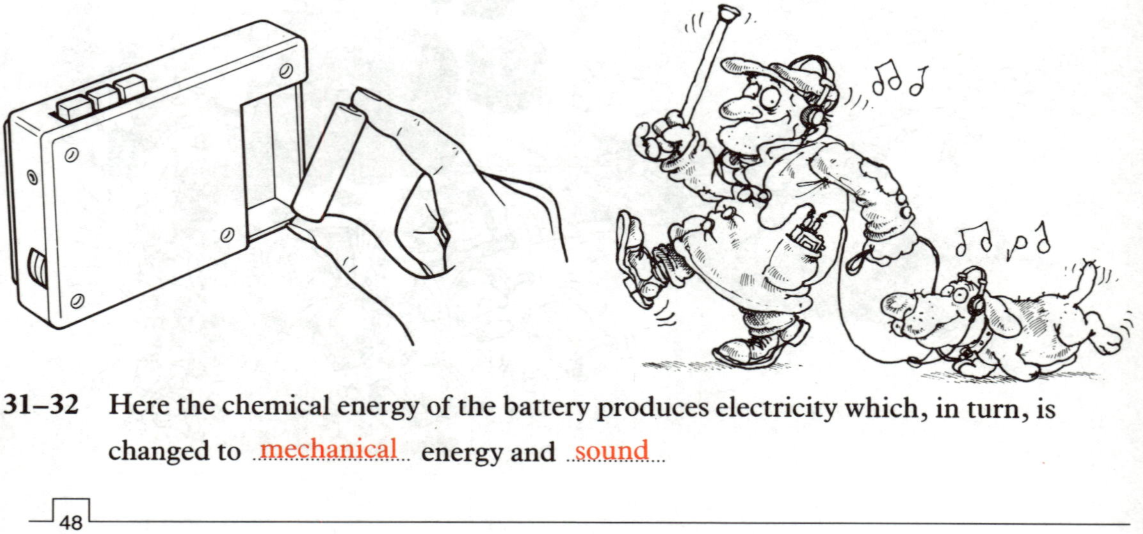

31–32 Here the chemical energy of the battery produces electricity which, in turn, is changed to mechanical energy and sound

[33–43]
The following strip cartoon traces the changes of forms of energy involved in propelling an electric train. Can you tell which forms of energy are used?

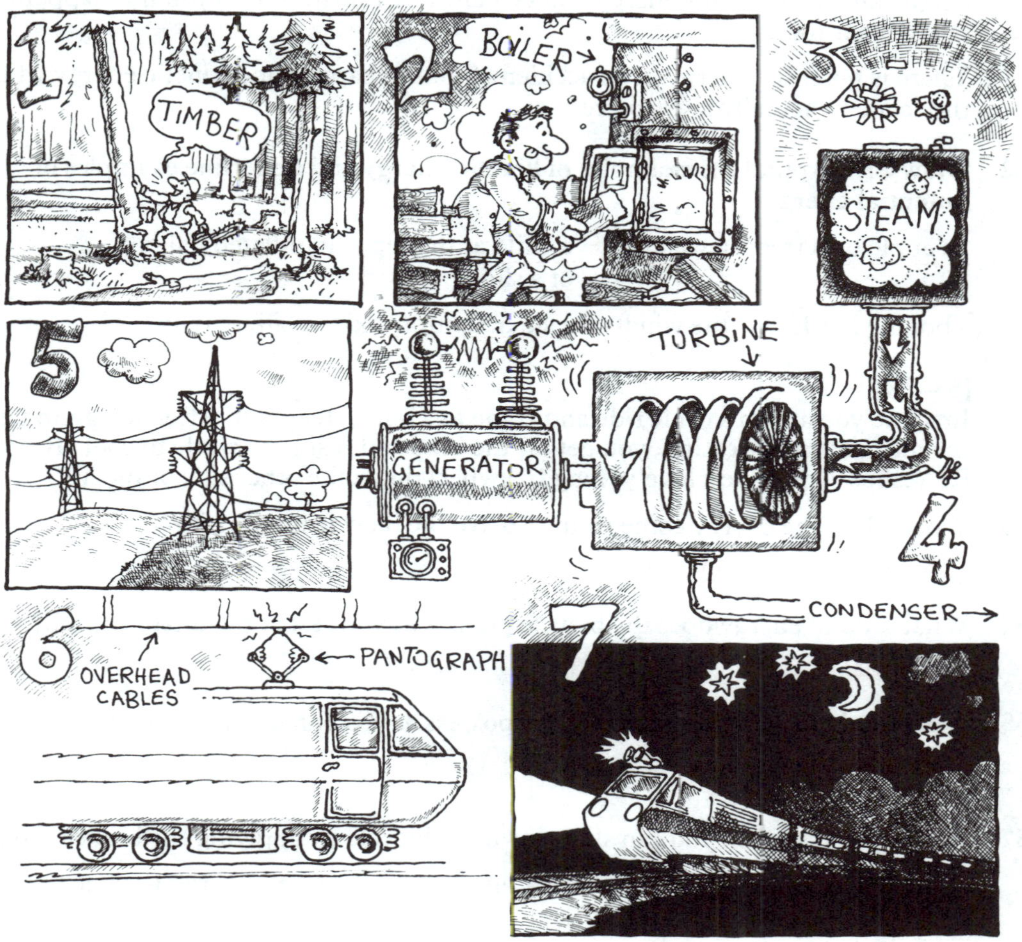

33–34 (1) shows ...solar... energy causing trees to grow and so make ...chemical... energy.

35–36 (3) shows wood being burnt turning ...chemical... energy into ...heat...

37–39 (4) shows the change of ...heat... into first ...mechanical... energy and then ...electrical energy...

40 (5) shows ...electrical... energy being transferred from place to place.

41–42 (6) shows ...electrical... energy being changed back into ...mechanical... energy.

43–44 What other forms of energy can you see in (7)? ...Light... and ...sound...

We can recognise differences between mechanical energy which is stored – **potential energy**, and active or **kinetic energy**. For example: a brick balanced on a post has potential energy, if it falls off the post the energy is released as kinetic energy and some of this energy will be painfully transferred to you if it happens to fall on your foot!

There is potential energy in an accident about to happen and kinetic energy when the accident actually takes place.

45–52 Draw a ring round the examples of **kinetic energy** and underline examples of **potential energy**:

an apple on a tree | a waterfall | a child at the top of a slide | an inflated balloon

a boiling kettle | the wind | a skier about to ski | a falling rock

[53–58]
Imagine you are on a cycle ride and come to a long, steep hill. After struggling up the hill, hot and sweating, you get off the bike and rest for a while to cool off. Refreshed, you have a lovely, long freewheel down the other side of the hill.

53 Where does the energy come from to drive the bicycle up the hill?

The muscles of the cyclist

54 What kind of energy does the bicycle possess as you rest at the top of the hill?

Potential energy

55 What kind of energy does the bicycle possess as you run down the hill?

Kinetic energy

56–57 On the run downhill you can slow down the bicycle by applying the brakes. Some of the bicycle's energy is absorbed in the brakes and this energy is given out as heat

58 However carefully you oiled it, some of the energy used to drive the bicycle up the hill is wasted as heat

[59–60]
Some of the ways in which energy can change its form are easier to understand than others.

59 Suppose we blow up a balloon and tie it off. If we measure its size and then place it near to a heater so that it gets warm what will happen to its size?

It will become larger

60 Why? Because heat energy makes the air in the balloon expand

[61–64]
Put a little water into a beaker, stretch a polythene bag over its neck, and hold it in place with a rubber band. Put the beaker on a hot plate, and place a 50p piece on the polythene bag. **YOU SHOULD ONLY DO THIS EXPERIMENT WITH THE HELP OF A PARENT OR TEACHER.**

61 What do you think will happen to the polythene bag as the water starts to boil?
It will be blown up

62 Will the 50p piece be lifted? Yes

63 The heat energy of the hotplate is changed to mechanical energy.

64 What mechanical device uses this idea and has made an enormous contribution to the modern world? The steam engine

[65–69]
A large amount of energy is needed to build a house, to make the bricks, to move the bricks, to make walls from the bricks and to do the countless other things which are needed to complete the house.

Similarly, living things require energy to grow and build more of themselves.

65 Which part of these plants will receive the most sunlight? The leaves

66 Which part of the plant would you expect to collect the solar energy and use it?
The leaves

67 Which of the plants would you expect to collect light most evenly over its surface?
1

68 Which plant do you think would grow best in a cloudy, misty region? 4

69 If all these plants get their energy from the sun, which parts collect the water and other building materials that they need? The roots

[70–73]
Some plants, especially trees, shed their leaves in the winter.

70 Can these plants collect solar energy in the winter? No

71 If not, how do you think that they will have the energy to grow new leaves in the spring? They will have stored energy

72 What could we do if we knew we would be unable to buy any food for some days or even weeks? We would buy extra food and store it

73 Can you suggest a plant, or kind of plant, that you know could do the same thing? Potato

74–80 Plants need energy to grow and ensure the species continues, by producing seed. Animals also need energy to grow and to **reproduce** – produce more of their own kind.

Animals cannot use the sun's energy directly for these purposes but must meet their essential energy needs by eating energy-rich foods.

Some animals are adapted to getting all their food and energy by eating plants – these are **herbivores**.

Other animals cannot easily meet all their food requirements by eating plants and they can only survive by hunting and eating other animals – these are **carnivores**.

[74–75]
All living things need energy to grow and reproduce

76 Herbivores also need energy to move around for the very large amounts of food they need.

77 Carnivores need more energy still to hunt their prey

78 Most humans are **omnivores**. An omnivore eats plants and animals

79 Can seeds of plants start to develop, or **germinate** in the dark, if they have no leaves to collect solar energy? Yes

80 If they can, where do you think they get the energy to germinate?
From chemical energy stored in the seed

PAPER 6 THE PROCESSES OF LIFE

What is alive?

[1–5]
What is a living thing? Is it anything that moves? Is it anything that increases in size, or grows?

Is it anything that produces young in order to continue its kind?

Is it anything that reacts to some kind of irritation or stimulation?

But first, is everything that uses energy alive?

1 A log rolls down a hill, moving faster and faster. Is it alive? No

2 A river rushes down to the sea, increasing in size and ferocity as heavy rains fall from the sky. Is it alive? No

3 As the swollen river rushes down to the sea in a storm, new rivulets and minor streams are sometimes formed temporarily. Is the river alive? No

4 Has the river produced 'young' to continue its kind? No

5 Ice reacts to heat by changing its form and melting. Is it alive? No

[6–12]
Read the following statements and answer with either **true or false:**

6 Every living thing has some ability to move itself. False

7 All living things grow at some time in their life. True

8 Every living thing produces young. False

9 Every kind of living thing can produce young.
False (some cross-breeds are infertile, for example, mules

10 All living things are sensitive to light. False

11 Different living things are more sensitive to some stimuli than to others. True

12 All living things consume energy. True

[13–24]
When we say that something is alive, we usually expect that it will move, it will grow, it will produce young, and it will react to stimulation by showing sensitivity to light, touch, temperature changes, noise, etc.

Underline those of the following that are alive:

crystals car water <u>tree</u> <u>leaf</u> storm

<u>rabbit</u> puppet fire <u>tadpole</u> <u>tiger</u> <u>fungus</u>

Circle those that are not alive, and list your reasons.

CRYSTALS do not consume energy or reproduce themselves

CAR does not reproduce or find its own energy

WATER does not consume energy or reproduce

STORM does not consume energy or reproduce

PUPPET does not consume energy, move itself or reproduce

FIRE is a chemical process rather than a material being

[25–30]
Is movement in plants and animals the same? No How do they differ? Give as many differences as you can. Animals can change location without growing. Plants can only move with the wind or by growing towards water, light or warmth

[31–35]
There are many different ways of producing young.

The general rule seems to be that the simpler the species, the larger the number of offspring, although like all rules there are exceptions.

Some species produce only one offspring after many months of development.

Mammals usually take the longest, from a few weeks to nearly two years, to produce the smallest number of babies.

31–34 Name four different kinds of living things that lay eggs?

Reptile, bird, insect, fish

35 Do egg-layers look after their children? (all do, some do, most do).

[36–37]
Among animals, the usual method of reproduction requires two different kinds of the species, a male and a female.

Among many plants, there is also a 'male' part of the plant, and a 'female' part of the plant. Sometimes they both exist in the same plant, sometimes different plants of the species develop as either male or female.

36 Plants usually reproduce by making seeds

There are other kinds of plant reproduction, however.

37 In what other ways can a plant reproduce itself?

Spores, bulbs, tubers, rhizomes, layering

A living thing, whether plant or animal, must feed in order to obtain energy for its life processes.

A living thing changes its food before it can use it.

Some of the food is burnt to provide energy, and this requires oxygen from the air and produces carbon dioxide. Breathing in air and breathing out carbon dioxide is part of **respiration**.

Feeding is necessary for growth. After feeding and respiration, the living thing has to get rid of the poisonous wastes left over from using its food. We call getting rid of this waste **excretion**.

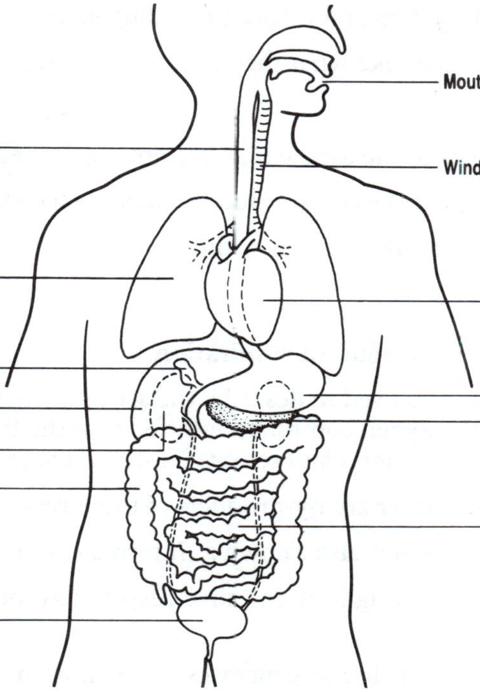

[38–51]

Fill in the blanks in the paragraphs below using these words:

excreted	**stomach**	**eliminated**	**hunger pangs**	**mouth**
small intestine	**gullet**	**kidneys**	**gastric juices**	**energy**
large intestine	**blood**	**saliva**	**food**	

Let us see what happens during a typical human meal.

Regularly, usually three times a day, your stomach sends messages indicating that it is time for the body to 'refuel'.

The messages normally take the form of ...hunger pangs... . You eat a meal. (We hope it is a healthy, nutritionally balanced meal!)

The food enters the body through your ...mouth... . Here it meets the first chemicals in your ...saliva... which will prepare it for use by your body.

First by chewing in your mouth and later, by the action of various chemicals, much of the ...food... is broken down into extremely small bits, many of which can dissolve in liquid.

As it travels down your ...gullet... to your ...stomach..., the food is mixed with more chemicals known as ...gastric juices...

Once dissolved, these bits of food are carried by your ...blood... to various parts of your body, which then take what they need for ...energy... for growth, and to store for future use.

If there are any parts of the food which are not used, these are ...excreted... from the body. If digestion produces by-products which are harmful, these are then ...eliminated... through the ...kidneys..., the ...small intestine... and ...large intestine...

[52–58]

Most living things show signs of **respiration**.

The word respiration is used to describe the series of chemical reactions in the plant or animal, in which oxygen combines with food (in the form of carbohydrates or fats), to break down the food and release its stored energy.

Carbon dioxide and water are by-products of these reactions and are breathed out.

This kind of **respiration** is also known as internal respiration or tissue respiration.

The simple act of breathing is often called respiration, but is more correctly called **ventilation**.

Plants and animals have similar processes of respiration.

In addition, plants take in carbon dioxide from the air, and water and some important minerals through the roots.

The plant has special parts of its green leaves, **chloroplasts**, containing chlorophyll, which use the energy of sunlight to make new energy-rich chemicals from the carbon dioxide and water, giving off oxygen.

This process is called **photosynthesis.**

These energy-rich chemicals are stored until needed and, when the plant needs energy, to keep alive, grow and develop, or to reproduce, the process of **respiration** takes place.

The ways in which plants and animals **respire** and the ways in which plants carry out **photosynthesis** show enormous variety, but are basically the same.

52 Do both plants and animals respire? ...Yes...

Underline the best answer:

53 The purpose of respiration is to (use the sun's energy, make new chemicals, release the energy in foods).

54 Both plants and animals carry out photosynthesis. (true, false)

55 Respiration uses oxygen. (true , false)

56 Photosynthesis produces oxygen. (true, false)

57 Photosynthesis uses carbon dioxide. (true, false)

58 Energy can be stored as energy-rich foods. (true, false)

Cells

All living organisms are composed of **cells**. This is the 'unit' of the living organism. These cells are often highly specialised ones, even in a plant or animal which seems quite simple.

We often refer to the single-celled plant or animal as the *simplest* of its kind, but when we examine even a single-celled organism, we soon see how very complicated it really is.

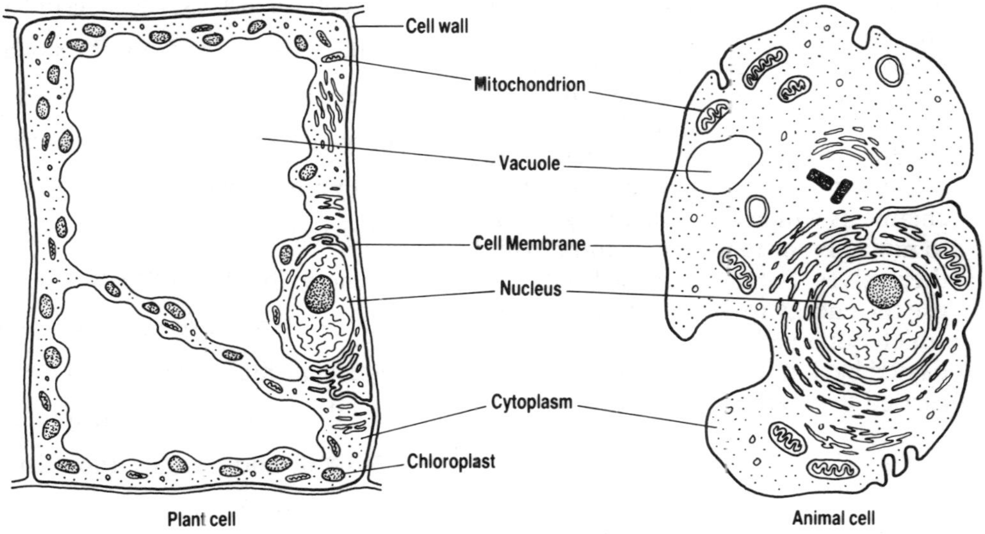

There are no typical cells, but there are similarities one can see in all cells.

All cells have a membrane, a flexible surrounding which contains the parts of the cell and allows various substances to get into the cell and to leave the cell.

Plant cells have an extra firm **cell-wall**, made of cellulose, which becomes stiffer with age, and provides the plant with a basis of support. In the animal world, shells or skeletons have the same role.

Inside the cell are different parts, which enable the cell to carry out its role as a tiny 'chemical processing factory'.

These include, the **nucleus** which contains all the plans and information which the cell needs to reproduce and the **mitochondria** where much of the complicated chemistry of the cell takes place.

In a single-celled animal or plant, the one cell performs all the chemical exchanges which enable the organism to take in energy (directly from the sun – in plants, or as food – in animals), to release the energy enabling it to grow, to reproduce, to excrete poisonous wastes, to react and to move.

In more complicated animals and plants, cells have become very specialised, so that each kind of cell performs a special task. It is a highly specialised chemical factory.

Animal and plant cells compared

[59–69]
Fill in the blanks using words which can be found in the paragraph on the left:

ANIMAL CELLS
need energy in the form of chemicals obtained from food, which is often obtained from plants. These chemicals are carried in the blood to the cells where they are absorbed across the cell membrane. Once inside the cells they are processed by the mitochondria to produce the energy the cell needs. The cells use the energy to make the new chemicals which they need for growth, to multiply, or to maintain and repair themselves. Some specialised cells also use the energy to make new chemicals which other cells need, and these are passed back out into the blood and carried to where they are needed.

PLANT CELLS
also need ...energy.... When light is falling on the leaves, the cells of the leaf use the light energy from the sun and carbon dioxide from the air to make energy-rich chemicals, by a process called **photosynthesis**. Some of these energy-rich chemicals are turned back into energy by the ...mitochondria... of the leaf cells and used to ...make... new chemicals which are required for ...growth..., when cells ...multiply..., or to ...maintain... and ...repair... the existing cell. Some of the energy-rich chemicals move out of the leaf ...cells... and are carried by the **sap** to the roots, where they are used to provide energy, or in some ...plants... like the potato, to be stored until ...needed... for new ...growth... in the spring.

[70–76]

Imagine that you could keep a day's diary for a human baby – and a one-celled animal like an amoeba.

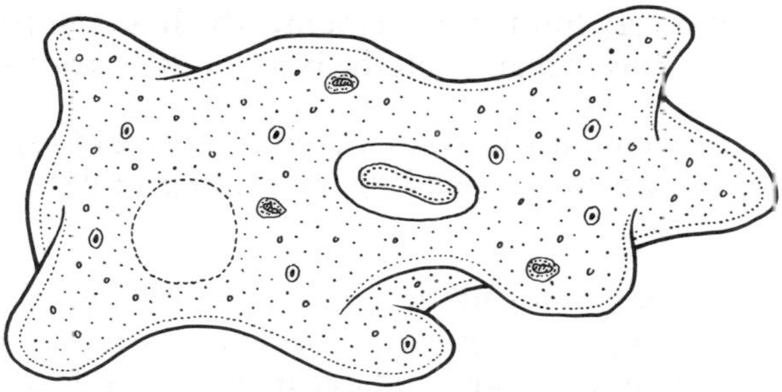

Amoeba, with nucleus

Morning: the young human aged eighteen months wakes up. The amoeba has been active all night. This is not insomnia, the amoeba may not sense much difference between day and night in its watery surroundings.

The toddler **eats** breakfast cereal, and drinks juice and milk.

The amoeba has a leisurely swim in its usual watery environment, constantly **eating** by flowing round and encircling particles of food, digesting them, and **excreting** poisonous wastes from various parts of its surface. This goes on continuously.

The toddler will eat lunch and supper, and dirty several napppies throughout the day. Some mothers will say that this happens all the time. In fact it does. The digestion of food goes on continuously; the excretion is gradually brought under control as the child is toilet-trained.

There is one important difference between the 'simple' animal and the more complicated one: the behaviour of the amoeba never changes – it will do the same thing in the same limited way for its whole life.

The more complicated animal, with its special organs for taking in, digesting and excreting its food, is **adaptable**. It can learn, and its cells can learn, different ways of behaving.

Both the amoeba and the toddler take in oxygen; the amoeba from its watery surroundings, and the toddler by breathing air. This is known as **respiration**.

Both of them take in food. The amoeba's cell, and specialised cells in the toddler's body both break the food down in order to release energy, and both use oxygen to do it.

Both the amoeba and the baby use this energy to grow, repair damaged parts, move about, react to stimulation, carry out respiration, feeding and excretion.

The amoeba will split when it reaches a certain size. The baby will become an adult before sharing with another adult the beginning of a new life: the birth of their baby.

Both will react to stimulation, and will move.

The difference is that the amoeba, as a single-celled animal, has a very limited range of reactions, and very limited movement, which is confined to flowing towards or away from objects mainly on the basis of their acidity.

The human baby will eventually have an incredible range of reactions, and an enormous range of movements (depending on training), by the time it is fully-grown.

An amoeba seems to have a 'built-in' best or maximum size; when it reaches this size, it simply begins to reproduce in what appears to be a most convenient system. It grows and grows, begins to divide, and eventually reproduces by becoming two identical, smaller, daughter cells instead of one large amoeba.

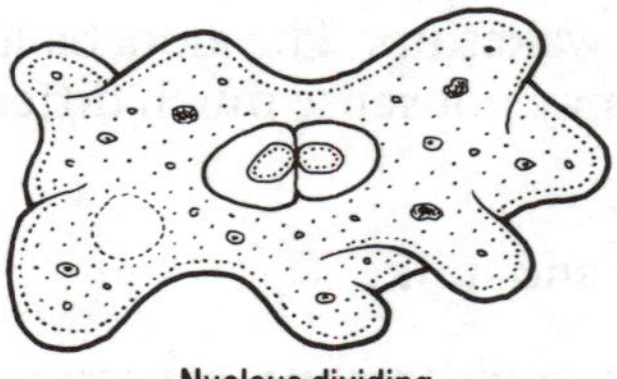

Nucleus dividing

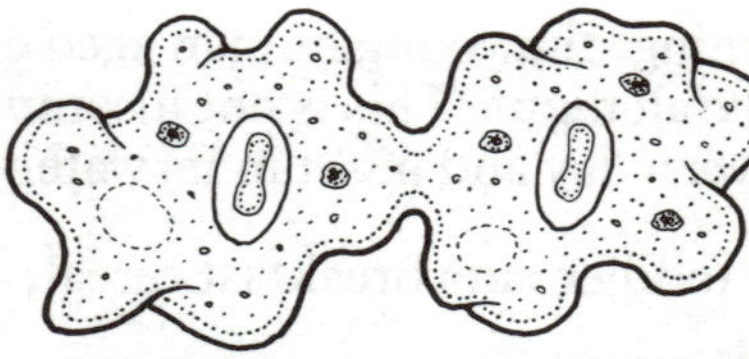

Nucleus divided and the Amoeba dividing

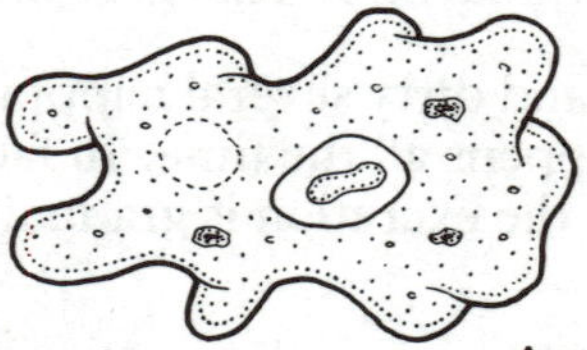

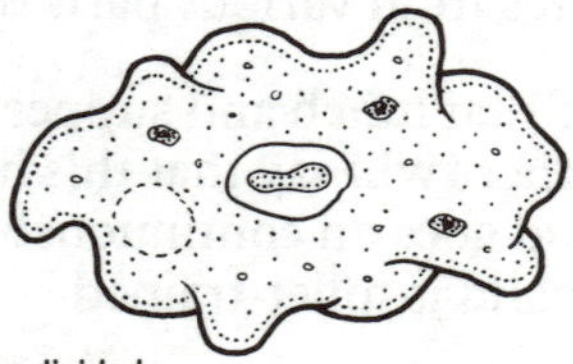

How Amoebas reproduce

Amoeba divided

The human baby will grow to maturity before it is ready to find a mate and produce babies of its own. Human babies need the care and attention that only adults can give.

Despite the limitations of the amoeba, it must be remembered that although single-celled, it is not really simple.

70 In a complicated animal like a human baby, are all the cells that make up the baby the same? No

71 How does the amoeba move? It flows

72 How does the amoeba take in its food? It flows around and encircles it

73 How do plants hold themselves up? By the stiffness of their cell walls

74 What gives the human baby shape and support? Its skeleton and muscles

75 Does the amoeba need oxygen? Yes

76 How does the human baby get rid of its poisonous waste products? Excretion

How to look after yourself

[77–90]
Fill in the gaps in the paragraphs below using these words:

epidemic cleanliness survive cancer pure shorter medicine ignorance electricity smoking quality germs disease exercise

Science has helped us to understand the importance of keeping clean. We know that g...erms... cause many diseases, that dirt harbours many germs, and that vermin carry d...isease... . We know that flies and insects must be kept away from food because they transfer disease-causing dirt and germs from dirty places to food if they are allowed to.

We know that personal ...cleanliness..., especially in the handling of food can make the difference between a long and healthy life and a short and diseased one. Unfortunately, there are still areas in the world where poverty and ...ignorance... result in many unnecessary deaths, especially among infants and children. Food handling also involves knowing how to cook it safely and how to store it safely, so that food poisoning does not occur.

A ...pure... and safe water supply is taken for granted by most people in Britain today, but, as recently as 70 years ago, a great cholera e...pidemic... which was caused by bad sanitary conditions and impure water supplies, swept through Europe, killing a very large number of people.

Doctors and scientists know that people who have regular ...exercise... and rest are likely to be fitter. People who are taught early in life how to protect themselves sensibly against disease and extremes of weather, and how to cope sensibly with everyday accident hazards, from traffic to dealing safely with ...electricity..., to taking medicines, are likely to ...survive... the longest.

Children (and adults) must learn to take only proper amounts of ...medicine... prescribed specifically for them. This same sort of sensible approach must be applied to other chemicals; whether they affect the body through smoking, which we know can cause ...cancer... and heart disease, or drinking alcohol or taking non-medicinal drugs.

Everything we take into our body should be considered for its usefulness and good effect on our long-term health and life. We ought to think carefully about whether we should subject our bodies to ...smoking... and 'drugs' at all, and consider the eventual harm to the length and quality of our life. Alcohol also needs to be considered. Taken in excess, it could also lead to a ...shorter... life of lower ...quality...

PAPER 7 LIGHT

Light and shade

[1–6]
Light is a form of energy to which our eyes are sensitive. The light that we are most familiar with comes from the sun. There are many sources of light, some natural and some man-made or artificial.

Give five examples of things which produce light.

1 Sun .... 2 Electric lamps .... 3 Candles ....

4 Fire .... 5 Television ....

6 What else is common to all of them? Heat ....

Sources of light vary greatly in brightness, from the lighted match which can only be seen up to a few metres away, to the sun which provides an immense amount of light on the earth at the incredible distance of 150 million kilometres.

If the sun is shining brightly we notice shadows.

Why can we see no shadows when it is cloudy?

To answer the question we need to understand what a shadow is, by asking some more questions and answering them.

[7–11]

7 Is a shadow an area which is not illuminated by the bright light? Yes ....

8 Is the area not illuminated because the object making the shadow obstructs the light? Yes ....

9 Does light only travel in straight lines? Yes ....

10 If we can answer all these questions we ought to understand why we cannot see shadows on a cloudy day, and why an electric lamp produces clear shadows while a fluorescent tube only gives slight and very fuzzy shadows.

Explain why this is:

A beam of light from a point of light like a small lamp is obstructed by the object and so produces a sharp shadow. Light from a fluorescent lamp comes from a large area and produces overlapping shadows ....

11 In the following list of measuring instruments, underline the one which uses a shadow to make the measurement.

compass <u>sundial</u> ruler stopwatch alarm clock

How light travels

[12–16]
If we drop a ball to the ground it usually bounces up directly into our hand.

12 If we throw the ball at an angle to the ground, what does it do? It bounces up at the opposite angle to the angle at which it hit the ground

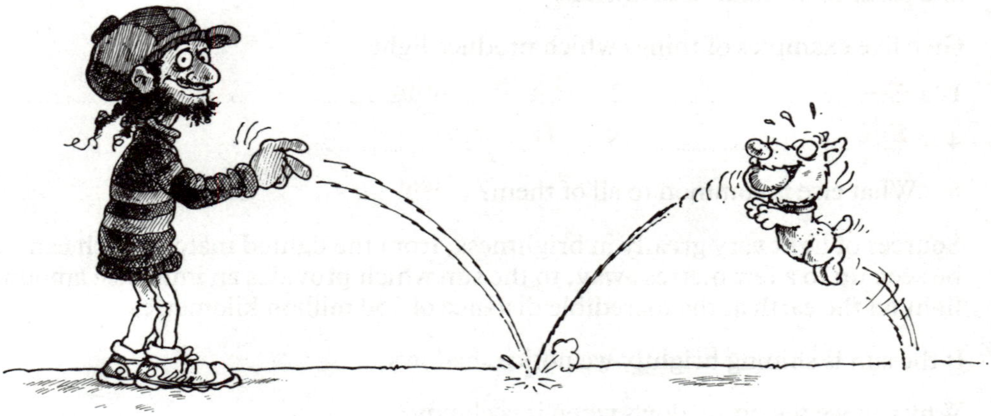

13 If you look directly into a mirror you can see yourself. If you look into the mirror at an angle will you still be able to see yourself? No

14 Will these two people be able to see each other? Yes

15 This proves that light travels in straight lines

Many of the measuring instruments that we use have pointers which move across a scale. Notice with kitchen scales how the reading you can make will vary as you move your eye from side to side. Accurate instruments often place a mirror behind the pointer.

16 Why is this? To ensure that we look at the scale vertically

[17–20]
Although light only travels in straight lines, we can see round corners if we use two mirrors.

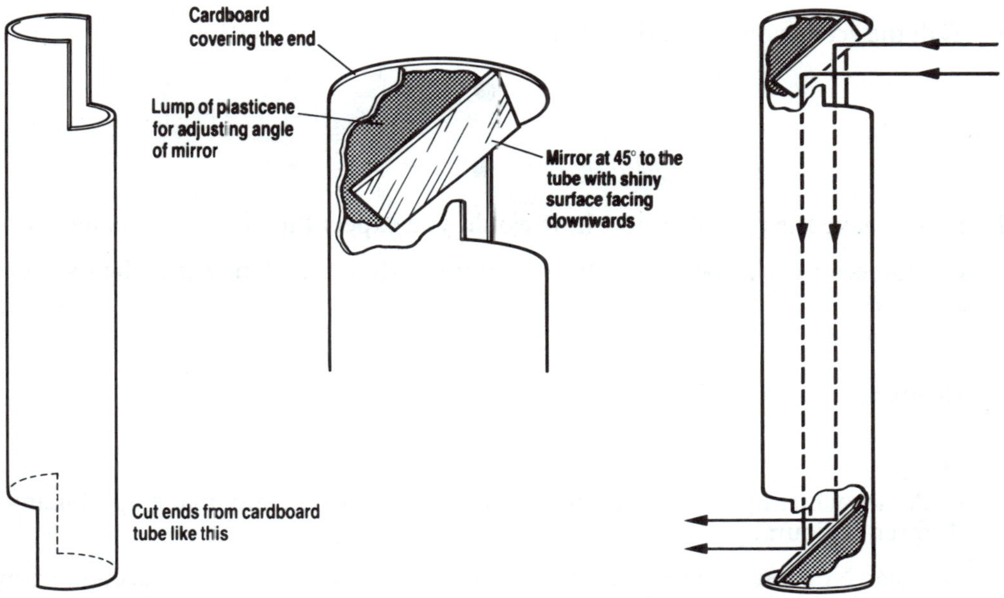

A similar arrangement is used on submarines to see above the surface when the craft is under water.

17 Do you know what this device is called? A periscope

You can make a simple device which tells us much about the way a camera works.

Take a shoe box and paint the whole of the inside black so that no light is reflected and then cut a small square out of each end.

Cover one of these squares with a piece of aluminium foil with a small hole pierced in the centre with a needle.

Then cut a piece of card to fit inside the box and cut out a large square in its centre.

Glue tracing paper to this square and glue this to the inside of the box.

Replace the lid, which has also been painted black on its underside.

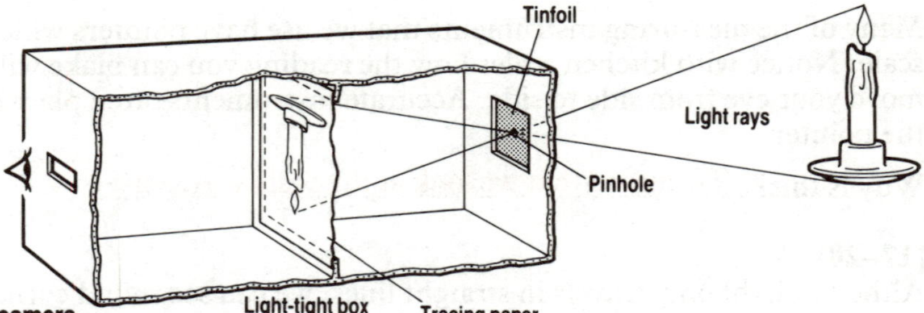

A homemade pinhole camera

If you hold up the box to a bright scene and look through the open hole you can see a picture of the scene on the tracing paper.

18 Will the scene you see be the right way up? No, it will be upside down

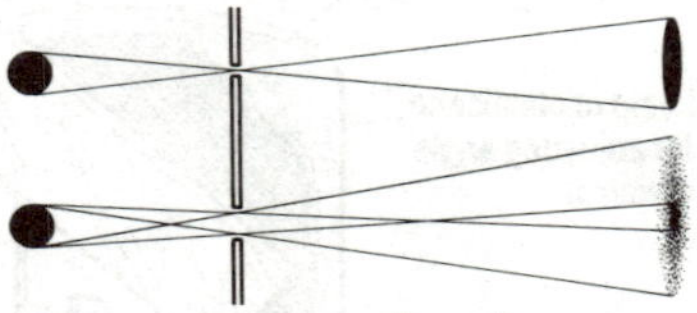

19–20 If you make the pinhole larger how would you expect the picture to change? It would become (sharper, more fuzzy, brighter, dimmer). Underline the two correct answers.

Colour

[21–28]
Ordinary white light from the sun or an electric bulb is really made up of many different colours.

Sir Isaac Newton, a great and famous scientist who lived three hundred years ago, noticed that glass chandeliers or diamonds which have been specially cut shine with many colours, although the light shining on them appears to be white.

To investigate this he closed all the shutters in his room to make it dark and then made a small hole in the blind to allow a ray of sunshine to come through.

He then arranged that the ray of light passed through a triangular piece of glass called a prism and then fell on a white screen.

He found that the ray of white light was split up into a **spectrum** showing coloured bands of red, orange, yellow, green, blue and violet.

Sir Isaac Newton experimenting with a ray of light and a prism

In the spectrum we do not find sharp edges to the coloured bands but they gradually shade from one colour to the next, so that we can see that about a third of the spectrum is mainly red, the middle third is mainly green and the remaining third is blue.

Red, green and blue are called the primary colours and if they are mixed again, white light will result.

Blue shades into violet and then into ultra-violet, which we cannot see.

Similarly, there is more light beyond the dark red which is called the infra-red, but again the eye is **insensitive** to infra-red light.

21 Can you think of anything occuring naturally, which causes white light to be split up into a spectrum? Rainbows

22 What do you think would happen to the spectrum if you placed a piece of red glass, or even a red toffee paper, in the beam of sunlight in Newton's experiment?

We would only see a red band

23 How would a piece of green glass in the beam of sunlight affect the spectrum?

We would only see a green band

In each case the coloured glass **subtracts** part of the light.

24 If you point three torches at the same piece of paper, one torch being covered with red glass, a second torch with green glass and the third torch with blue glass, what colour will the paper appear?

White

Here the different colours are being **added** together.

25 The red glass allows red light to pass through and blocks the other colours.

A material which allows light to pass through it is called **transparent**.

If it blocks the light it is said to be **opaque**.

–28 The blue glass is transparent to blue light and opaque to other colours.

[29–33]
We see objects by the light that is reflected from them, so, if we view a coloured picture in a darkened room with a red light the red parts of the picture will show up and the rest of the picture will be dark.

29 The red parts of the picture reflect red light.

If we examine the picture in white light the

30 blue parts will reflect blue light and

31 green parts will reflect green light.

32 We can make an experiment to see this in a slightly different way.

Take a circular piece of card and divide it up into six equal segments.
Colour each of these segments as brightly as possible.

Push a pencil through the centre of the coloured wheel and you have made a top.
Now spin the top.

If the top is spinning fast enough your eye will no longer be able to see the individual segments and the spinning disc will appear nearly ...white...

33 Are we seeing the three reflected colours added together? ...Yes...

At this point you may be fairly convinced that white light actually is a mixture of many colours but you still may not understand why a prism splits white light to form a spectrum as Sir Isaac Newton demonstrated.

We need to know a little more!

Refraction of light

[34–35]
Take a bowl of water and hold a straight ruler in the water at an angle of about 45°.

34 How does it look? ...Bent or curved...

Shine a torch which gives a pencil beam of light through a jar of water in a darkened room. You can see that the rays of light from the torch are bent as they pass into the water and then bend the opposite way as they emerge into the air again.

35 This shows that light rays ...bend... when they pass from air into a different transparent substance.

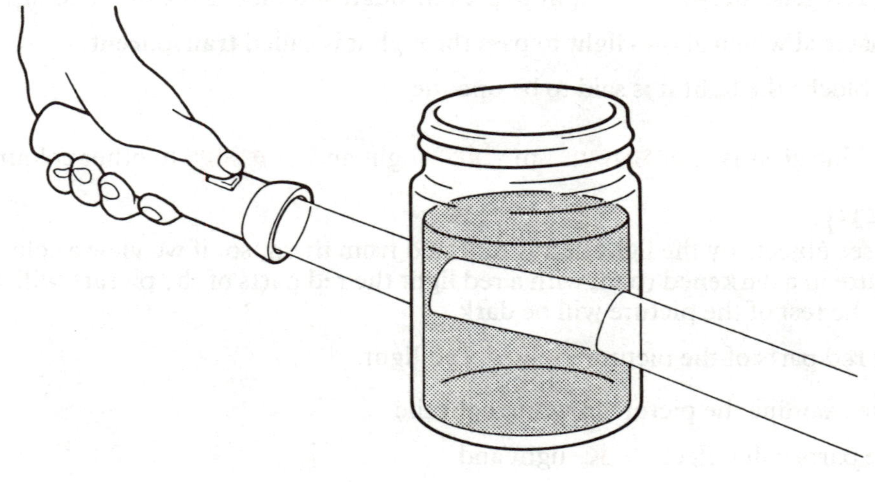

[36–42]
This effect is called **refraction**.

Fill in the blanks in the paragraphs below using these words:

beam fast shadows light hot slowed white

Although light rays travel incredibly ...fast... they are ..slowed.. down slightly in transparent solids or liquids.

Light also travels faster through warm air than cold air, and on a hot day we can notice that the ..light... shimmers above a hot road, as currents of ...hot... air rise from the road.

You can also see the same effect with a strong torch in a darkened room, when the torch is shone at a ..white... wall with the ..beam... passing just above a candle flame; producing twisting patterns and ...shadows...

43 You can see things because they do something to the light which falls on them. Solid objects reflect light so that we can see them; they also obstruct light so we can see their shadows. Transparent substances such as glass also reflect some of the light so that we can see reflections in windows. Can you ever see air? ...Yes...

[44–51]
Fill in the blanks using words from this list:

white prism slowest bend speeds transparent colours differ

As we have seen, ...white... light is a mixture of ...colours. and the different colours all travel at slightly different ...speeds... blue light is the fastest, green is slower, yellow is slower still and red light travels the ...slowest... The various colours will all ...bend... when they pass from air into another ...transparent... substance such as glass, and because they are travelling at different speeds the amount they bend will ...differ..., so we can begin to understand Sir Isaac Newton's experiment with the ...prism... .

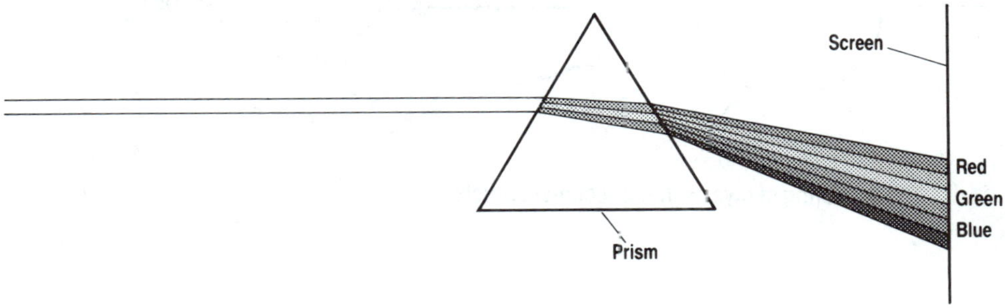

52 Why does cut-glass sparkle with different colours? It bends or refracts the light

Some transparent materials slow down light more than others and so they cause the light to bend more. They are said to have a high **refractive index.**

53 Would you expect such materials to produce a wider spectrum in Newton's experiment? Yes

54 Diamonds are very much prized for the way they flash with many colours. Would you expect diamonds to have a very high refractive index? Yes

55 Would you think that the sparkle and colours depend on the way the diamond is cut? Yes

[56–63]
The following is a list of gems: underline the ones which depend on refraction for their beauty, and ring the ones which depend more on their colour or reflection.

pearl emerald topaz diamond ruby sapphire turquoise agate

Scattering

[64–71]
On a very clear day sunlight seems to come to us almost uninterrupted.

If it is cloudy many of the rays of sunlight encounter droplets of water in the clouds and much of the light is deflected by the droplets.

Then, instead of all the light coming directly from a point in the sky (the sun) the light appears to come from a very large area and is **diffuse.**

This interception and deflection of light rays is known as **scattering.**

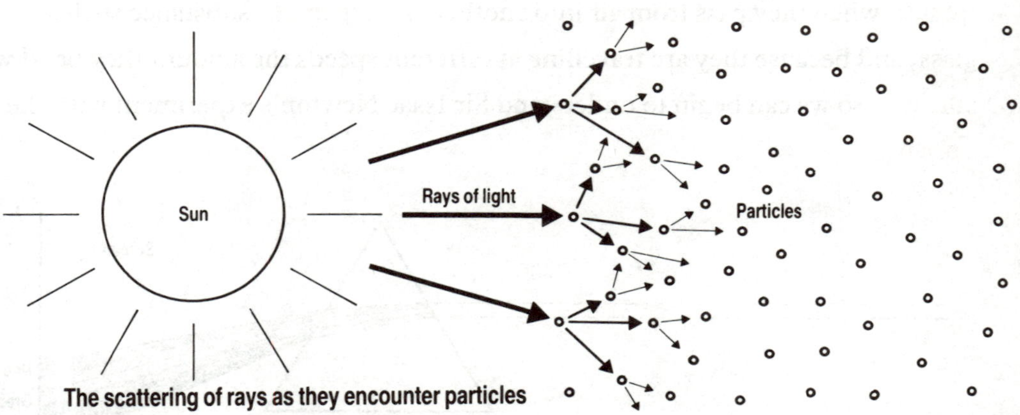

The scattering of rays as they encounter particles

Not all colours of light are scattered by the same amount. Blue is deflected more than green or red.

During the day when the sun is high more blue light is deflected towards the earth so that the sky looks blue.

In the early morning or late evening the sun is low in the sky and sunlight has to pass through more of the earth's atmosphere to reach us. If we look at the sun then, because more of the blue and violet has been deflected away from us, the sun appears to be red.

64 When does sunlight come to us most directly through least atmosphere?

At midday

65 What can rays of sunlight encounter? Water droplets and dust

66 What happens to the sunlight when it encounters a cloud? It is scattered

67 What colours of light are deflected most? (blue, green, yellow, red)
Underline the correct answer.

68 When does the sky appear at its most blue? Midday

69 The sun appears reddish (at late evening, midday, on a clear day).
Underline the correct answer.

70 After a hot dry day when the air is dusty we often get a brilliant red sunset. Why might that be? More of the blue light is deflected away leaving the red

71 What does **diffuse** mean? Spread out

[72–75]
Take two beakers of water and add a few drops of milk to one of the beakers and stir. Darken the room and shine a torch into each of the beakers from the top.

72 Which beaker would you expect to light up? The one with milk in it

73 Why is that? The droplets of milk will scatter the light

74 Why will the beaker which lights up look bluish? The blue light will be deflected towards you

75 If you shine the torch from the side why will the beaker which lights up show a reddish colour? The blue light will be deflected most leaving the red

PAPER 8 SOUND

Sound is always made by some kind of movement. Clapping your hands or plucking a guitar string makes sound, although the sounds are very different. If you put your finger gently against a ringing bell you can feel it vibrating. If you press harder you stop the vibrations and the sound.

[1–7]
When anything vibrates it makes a sound.

The energy of the moving (vibrating) object is passed on to the tiny particles of air making them move.

As these particles (**molecules**) of air move they jostle molecules next to them and the sound is carried further.

The stronger the vibrations, the more energy they give to the air and the louder the sound.

To make the air molecules move requires energy. The further the sound travels the more air molecules are affected and so the energy of the vibrations are used up; the sound dies away.

A vibrating tuning fork making ripples on water

These vibrations are called **sound waves**, you cannot see them but if you strike a tuning fork and dip the prongs of the fork into a glass of water the vibrations make a pattern of ripples on the water.

If you drop a pebble into a pool of water, you will notice that small ripples, or waves, spread out from where the pebble hit the water. These are rather like sound waves.

As the sound waves move through the air, they jostle successive particles, or **molecules**, of air.

The particles or molecules crowd together. Imagine a dense crowd of people, like those at a parade. If several at the front are pushed back by the police they in turn push against the ones behind them and a ripple runs through the whole crowd.

This crowding together causes a slight increase in pressure. The molecules then move apart again and the pressure drops.

Our ears detect these small changes of pressure as the sound waves reach our ear drum, and so we hear sounds.

Vibrations are also transmitted through solid objects where the molecules of the object successively bounce against each other.

The vibrating solid object eventually causes the air next to it to vibrate and so it is always the vibration of the air that we actually hear.

1 Sound waves are like ripples in the air

2 Sound waves are produced by vibrations

3 Can sound waves travel through empty space? No

4 What do our ears detect as sound? Vibrations in the air

5 What decides how far a sound will travel in air? The loudness of the sound, or the violence of the original vibrations

6 Do all sounds have the same quality? No

7 Are all sounds pleasing to listen to? No

[8–13]

Because sound waves travel by causing molecules of air or other materials to bounce against each other, sound waves travel much slower than light waves, and they travel at different speeds according to the nature of the material that they pass through.

Sound travels faster through dense materials such as glass, steel or water than it does through air.

In dense materials the molecules are closer together than they are in air and so the sound is carried faster.

Sound travels at about 1200 kilometres per hour in air, or about 330 metres per second. It travels at over four times this speed in water, and nearly 15 times as fast in steel.

By comparison, light waves travel at almost 300,000 kilometres a second, which is over 100,000 times as fast.

8 You are watching a cricket match from the back of a large stand which is about 200 metres from the pitch. Will you hear the batsman strike the ball (at the same time as, before, after) you see him make the stroke? Underline the correct answer.

9 In a thunderstorm you see a bright flash of lightning, if it takes 10 seconds before you hear the clap of thunder; how far away was the lightning? 3300 metres

[10–13]

Imagine that you and a friend have a noisy firework (which also produces a bright flash) and a stop watch, and that you are near to two convenient hills which are a known distance apart. Describe how you could measure the speed of sound by filling in the gaps below.

Step 1 One person takes the stop watch to one hill and the second person takes the firework to the top of the second hill.

10 Step 2 The firework is lit

11 Step 3 The stopwatch is started when the firework flash is seen

12 Step 4 The stopwatch is stopped when the firework bang is heard

13 Step 5 The distance is divided by the number of seconds between the flash and the bang to give the speed of sound in metres per second

[14–15]

If strong sound waves strike a hard surface it vibrates and it then produces further sound waves – the sound is reflected.

The reflected sound takes time to travel back and we hear it as an **echo** of the original sound.

In a valley among rocky cliffs we often get very good echoes. If we make a loud noise, or shout, the echo often comes back to us after several seconds.

The time difference between the original sound and the echo is the time taken for the sound to travel to the rock which reflects it and back again to our ear.

14 If the echo from a shout takes 4 seconds to return, how far away was the rocky cliff that it echoed from? 660 metres

15 If one shout produces several echoes one after the other; what might that mean?

The sounds are reflected from more than one place

[16–18]

When we listen to music in a hall, or try to listen to a teacher in a classroom, what we actually hear is changed by echoes from the walls of the room. Hard walls reflect a good deal of sound, soft materials such as curtains reflect very little.

The echoes are called **reverberations**, and the length of the echo is called the **reverberation time**.

If the hall or classroom is relatively large, the reflected sounds arrive back at our ears a few moments after the original sound.

If a classroom has a high ceiling made of hard material such as plaster it will tend to reflect all sorts of sounds, such as the scuffling of feet, and these reflections will add to the general noise and make it difficult for the teacher to hear clearly.

Acoustics is the study of sound and echoes. It helps us to understand what makes the sound qualities in some concert halls and theatres better than in others.

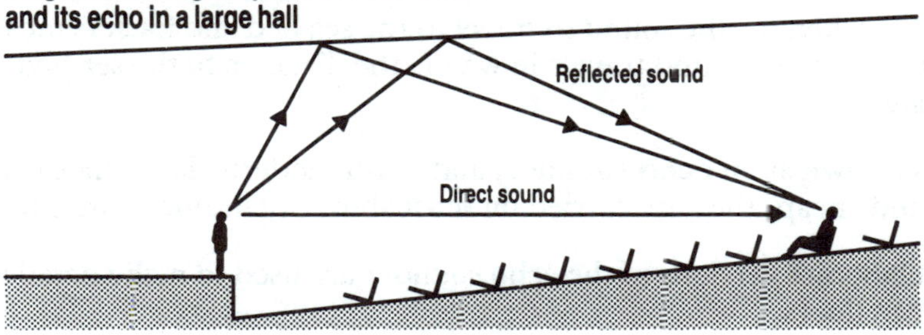

16 Why will a very large hall have a long reverberation time?

The sound has further to go to be reflected

17 Why does music played in the open air tend to sound thin and 'dead', compared with the same performance in a concert hall?

There are no reverberations

18 How could a hall be changed so that music played in it sounds more like it does out of doors?

By hanging soft coverings on the walls and ceilings to reduce echoes

[19–22]
Apart from improving the sound qualities of enclosed public places, echoes have proved very valuable for measuring distances.

One of the best examples of this is the equipment used to survey the depths of the seas and oceans.

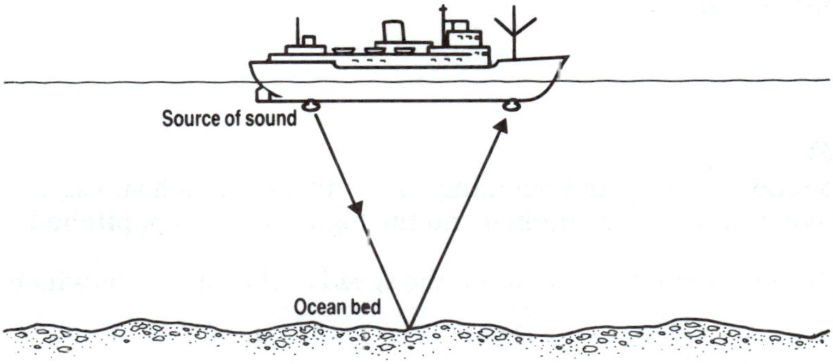

A device rather like an electronic bleeper is fixed to the bottom of the hull of a ship to direct the sound waves downwards.

The sound waves reflected from the sea bed are collected by a microphone on the hull of the ship.

The reflected signal is compared with the original one sent by the bleeper.

The time taken for the sound to travel to the sea bed and back is measured, and knowing how fast sound travels in water, the distance to the sea bed can be calculated.

This is known as an **echo sounder**, and, with modern electronics which make them small and cheap, they are carried on most ships, including quite small yachts.

More elaborate versions of the echo sounder are used to make detailed surveys of the ocean floors.

Other similar instruments are used in submarines to 'see' other ships while submerged. These are called **sonar**.

19 Small ships spend much of their time in coastal waters. Why is it particularly important for them to carry echo sounders?

So they can avoid running aground

20 Fishing vessels carry echo sounders for a rather special reason. Can you think why?

To detect shoals of fish

21 Some animals that live in the sea make great use of echoes in a similar way. These animals are (sharks, whales, cod, jellyfish). Underline the correct answer.

22 In nature, the use of echoes for 'seeing' and navigation is not just used by sea creatures. Can you think of an animal which uses echoes on land to 'see' in the dark? Bats

Qualities of sound

Pitch

[23–26]
Some sounds are deep and booming while others are high and squeaky. We call the deep boomy sounds **low pitched** and the high sounds **high pitched.**

The pitch of the sound depends on the speed of the vibrations which cause the sound.

23 Hold the end of a plastic ruler flat against a table or desk and make it vibrate by flicking the end. If a long length of ruler is free to vibrate, are the vibrations slow enough to see? Yes

24 Now shorten the length of ruler which is free to vibrate over the edge of the table. Does the pitch of the sound increase? Yes

–26 As you shorten the free end of the ruler more and more, does the pitch increase more and more? Yes Do the vibrations appear to be faster? Yes

Another way to demonstrate pitch is to attach a piece of cardboard to the fork of your bicycle so that it touches the spokes of the wheel. As you pedal the bicycle faster the pitch of the sound made by the cardboard becomes higher.

[27–30]
The speed of the vibrations which cause a sound is called the **frequency** and is measured in cycles per second. Middle C on the piano has a frequency of 256 cycles per second. Each cycle is a 'to and fro' movement of the vibration.

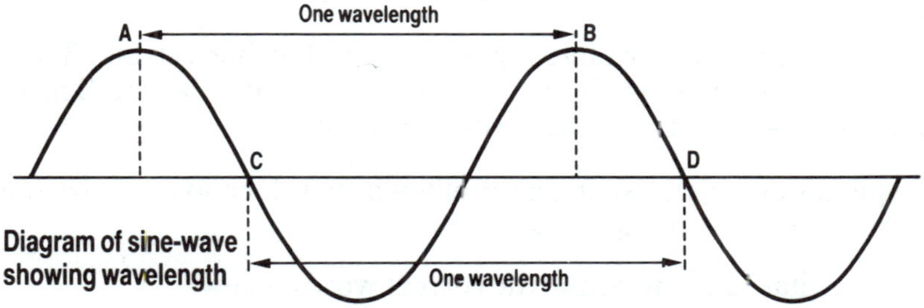

This diagram shows a sound wave, from A to B is one complete vibration, and it is called a **wavelength**.

As we have said, the speed of sound in air is about 330 metres per second. So if a sound has a frequency of 330 cycles per second, there will be 330 complete vibrations in 1 second, or 330 metres. Each vibration will be $\frac{330}{330} = 1$ metre long. This is its wavelength.

Notice that the vibrations have their maximum effect at points A and B and no effect at C and D.

27 What will be the wavelength of a sound that has a frequency of 660 cycles per second? $\frac{1}{2}$ metre

28 If a musical note has a wavelength of $\frac{1}{4}$ metre, what will be its frequency? 1320

–30 The wavelength of a particular musical note will be (longer, shorter, the same) in water than it is in air, and (longer, shorter, the same) in steel. Underline the correct answer.

This illustrates that, in science, changing one thing that can vary (**a variable**) often causes other things to change.

Resonance

[31–37]
Imagine that you are pushing your little sister on a swing. If you stand back and push her gently every time she reaches the highest point of her swing you will notice that relatively small pushes will make her swing higher and higher.

31 If you push her when she is near the bottom of the swing will it have as much effect? No

32 If you push her as she swings towards you will it have as much effect? No
The pushes are only effective if they are in rhythm or in **phase** with the swinging.

Sound waves are much the same. Everything has a **natural frequency** which is the frequency at which it vibrates naturally if disturbed in some way or another.

Striking a tuning fork causes it to vibrate at its natural frequency. Banging a gong produces a particular pitch which depends on the size of the gong.

Air can be set to vibrate by plucking, striking or bowing a string. The **loudness** of the sound depends on how violently you pluck, strike or bow it. The pitch which is produced depends on the characteristics of the string.

The frequency at which a string naturally vibrates depends on how long it is, how tightly it is stretched and how thick it is.

Examine a guitar, and underline the correct words below:

33 The low sounding strings are (thicker, thinner) than the high sounding strings.

34 Adjust the tuning to make a string tighter and pluck the string. Does tightening the string (increase, decrease) the pitch?

35 Pluck a string and then press the string to the fingerboard to shorten it. Does the pitch of the note (increase, decrease)?

36–37 So, on a piano, the strings that produce the bass notes are thicker and longer than the strings which produce the high notes.

[38–40]
Vibrating strings do not transfer much of their energy directly to the air, so to make a practical stringed instrument the vibrations of the strings need to be made to vibrate the air more efficiently.

This is done with a sounding board or box. The strings pass over a bridge which transfers the vibration of the string to a board or box, and this in turn vibrates moving a larger volume of air and making the sound louder.

A guitar string set in motion may vibrate 256 times a second which will sound the same pitch as middle C on the piano.

At the same time, the string may also vibrate in many parts. Each half of the string also vibrates twice as fast giving a sound of 512 cycles/second which is the C above middle C.

It may also vibrate in thirds or quarters of the string giving sounds which are higher again in pitch. These higher notes are called **overtones** or **harmonics** of the fundamental frequency.

They are normally weaker than the fundamental note, but it is the presence of these **harmonics** which give the musical notes their special quality which is characteristic of an instrument, and make a violin sound different from a guitar.

38 Why do stringed instruments need a soundboard or soundbox?

To cause more air to vibrate than can be produced by the strings.

39 Why are harmonics important? They add to the sound quality

40 Harmonics will be (a simple multiple, twice, half, a quarter) of the fundamental note. Underline the correct answer.

[41–43]

Like strings, enclosed columns of air have a natural frequency. This depends on the length of the column.

–42 Take three empty milk bottles: leave A empty, fill B half full of water, fill C three-quarters full of water. You can make the air in each of the bottles vibrate by blowing across the top of them. Which bottle will produce the lowest note and which bottle will make the highest sound?

Lowest A Highest C

This effect is known as **resonance** and the pitch at which an object, or volume of air **resonates** is known as the **resonant frequency**.

43 If plucking a guitar string makes it vibrate 2000 times every second, what is its resonant frequency? 2000 per second

[44–50]

Have you ever noticed, in a band or orchestra, that the low pitched sounds are made by large instruments, while the high sounds are made by small instruments?

The tuba is a very large metal instrument which has a very long coiled up pipe. The long column of air enclosed in this pipe makes very deep notes.

The trumpet has a much shorter length of tube and makes fairly high pitched sounds.

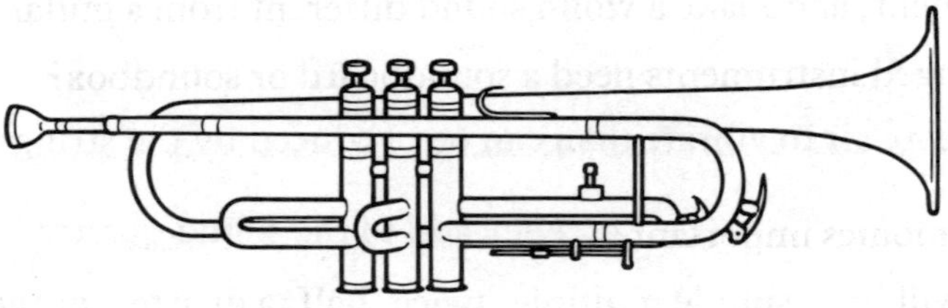
Trumpet

In wind instruments the air is set in motion (vibration) by blowing through the mouthpiece using various methods of making a high speed jet of air.
In trumpets, horns, trombones and tubas pursed lips provide a means of starting and sustaining the air in vibration.

The woodwind instruments such as the clarinet, saxophone, oboe and bassoon use wooden reeds shaped like sharp blades to give the air the necessary push.

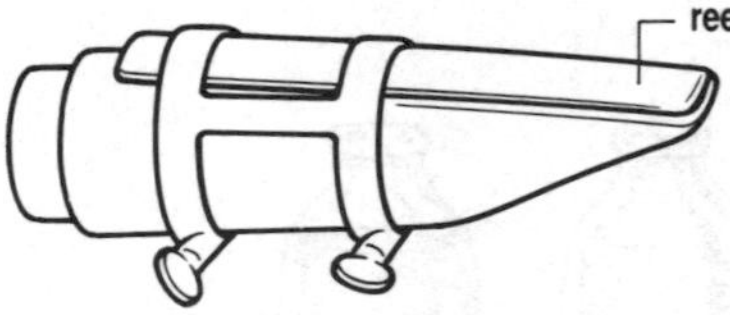

Clarinet mouthpiece

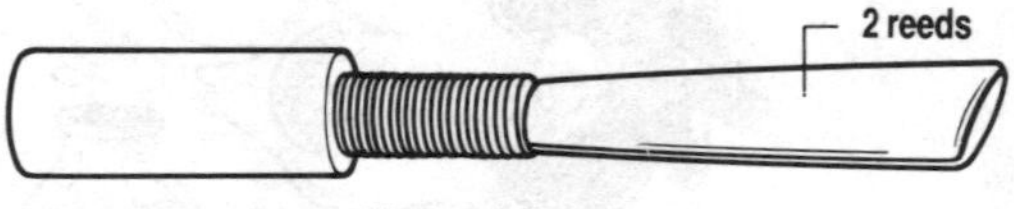

Oboe mouthpiece

Other woodwind instruments like the flute and piccolo are sounded by blowing across a hole with sharp edges.

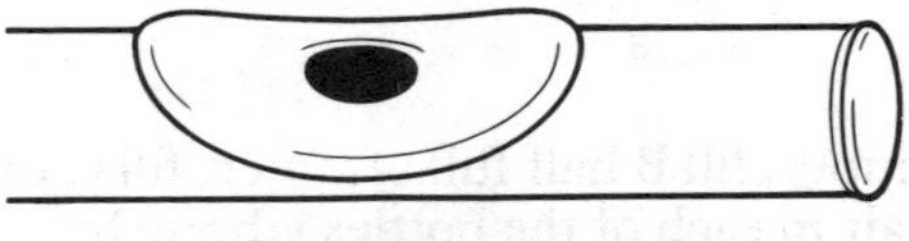
Flute mouthpiece

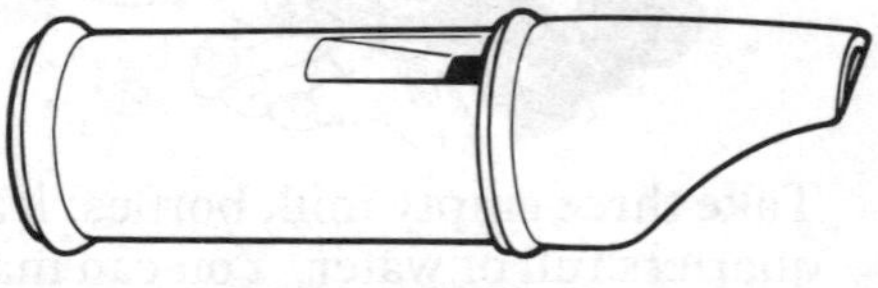
Recorder mouthpiece

All of these instruments produce notes of a pitch or frequency which is determined by the resonant frequency of the column of air. To vary the pitch requires changing the length of the air column.

Pitch is changed in trumpets, horns and tubas by adding extra pieces of pipe by means of valves. Trombones change pitch by using tubes which slide in and out to change the length of the air column.

You can change the pitch of woodwind instruments by stopping up holes in their tubes, either with the finger tips or with pads which are operated by keys.

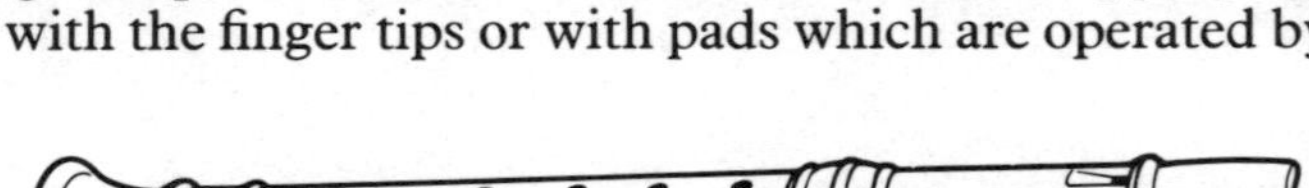
Recorder

In wind or woodwind instruments:

44 What decides on the pitch of a particular note? The length of the air column

45 How can the pitch be varied to make music? By stopping up the holes in the tube or altering the length of the tube

46 Would you call the recorder a woodwind instrument? Yes

How is the 'push' given to start the air vibrating:

47 in a clarinet? By blowing past a reed

48 in a trombone? By pursing the lips in a mouthpiece

49 in a flute? By blowing across a hole

50 in a trumpet? By pursing the lips in a mouthpiece

You will have noticed that a note played on a clarinet will have a quite different quality from the same note played on a trumpet, and these will both have a different sound from the same note played on a flute.

[51–57]
Fill in the missing words in the paragraphs below using these words:

vibrations metal frequency clarinet column resonate harmonics

The material of the musical instrument is set in vibration by the air column contained inside it and this in turn passes on the vibrations to the outside air. So the material enclosing the column of air is likely to add its own peculiarities to the quality of the sound.

Clarinets are usually made of wood, but some are made of metal. A metal clarinet has a much sharper, brighter sound than the mellow, sweet sound of a wooden one. But they both have the characteristic sound of a clarinet, so material is not the complete explanation.

An open column of air will resonate at a fundamental frequency and produce harmonics in the same way as a vibrating string. It is the presence of different amounts of these overtones or harmonics which give an instrument so much of its individuality.

[58–64]
We have seen that stringed instruments produce their sound by making strings vibrate and the pitch is controlled by the length, tightness and thickness of the string.

Wind instruments make sounds by the vibration of columns of air. The pitch is controlled by the length of the air column.

There is a third kind of instrument where the vibrations are caused by striking a solid object made of metal or wood.

In these instruments the pitch is controlled by the size and shape of the solid object and the nature of the material.

These are called **percussion** instruments and include bells, triangles, and xylophones.

You cannot change the shape and size of a percussion instrument to vary its pitch. In order to play a series of different notes using bells requires a whole set of bells of varying sizes – one for each note.

Each bell in a chime of bells and each bar on a xylophone has to be very accurately and precisely made to resonate at the exact pitch that is required of it.

Sound travels much faster in solids than it does in air so that the size of a xylophone bar or bell which resonates at a particular pitch is much shorter than the column of air in a wind instrument.

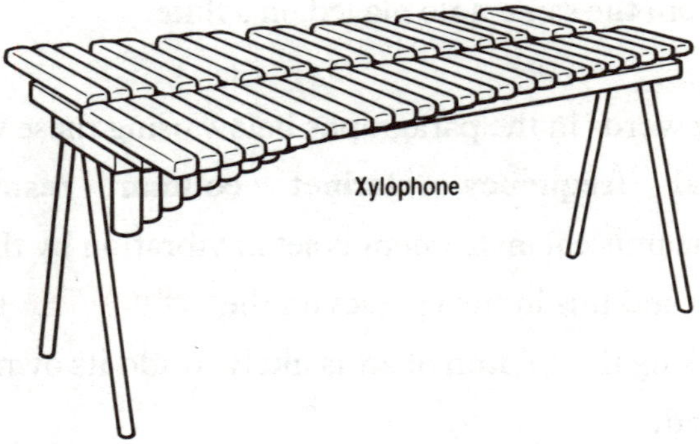

58 If the pitch of a bell is slightly lower than it should be, can you fairly easily alter the bell to raise it? Yes

59 If so, how? File a small amount of metal away

60 If the pitch is slightly higher than it should be, is there an easy way of lowering it? No

61 If so, how? Adding on metal is not easy

If the bar on a xylophone which sounds middle C on the piano is of a particular length, would the bar

62 which sounded the C below middle C be (longer, shorter)?

63 which sounded the C above middle C be (longer, shorter)?

Underline the correct answers

64 What other kind of percussion instrument can you think of which we have not mentioned? Drums

PAPER 9 MAGNETISM AND ELECTRICITY

Magnetism

People have known about magnetism and electricity for a very long time.

About 2500 years ago the ancient Greeks discovered that a certain kind of black stone was strange in that it attracted pieces of iron.

This black stone is called magnetite and is a form of iron ore. It is also called lodestone.

The common magnets that we see nowadays are made of iron or steel usually formed into a bar – a bar magnet; the bar is sometimes bent round in a horseshoe shape to make a horseshoe magnet, and button shapes or ring magnets are quite common.

[1–7]
If we take two bar magnets and place them close together side by side we will notice that one way they are pulled strongly together, while the other way they move apart.

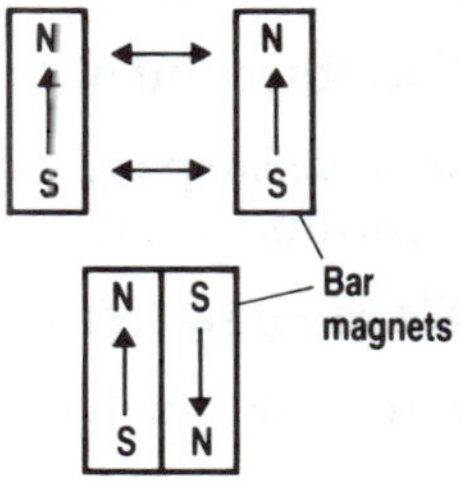

1 Do you think that the magnets are different at each end? Yes

If we hang up the bar magnets we will notice that they swing round to point in a particular direction. Mark the same direction on each magnet with an arrow.

2 Lay the magnets side by side with the arrows pointing in the same direction, will they be attracted or try to separate? They will try to separate

3 If they are placed with the arrows facing in different directions will they try to separate (be **repelled**), or be attracted? They will be attracted

4 What does this prove? Unlike ends of magnets attract each other and like ends repel each other

5 If we suspend one magnet and hold another one about 10 centimetres away from the first one at an angle of about 45° with the arrows pointing in opposite directions, what will happen?
It will swing towards the suspended magnet

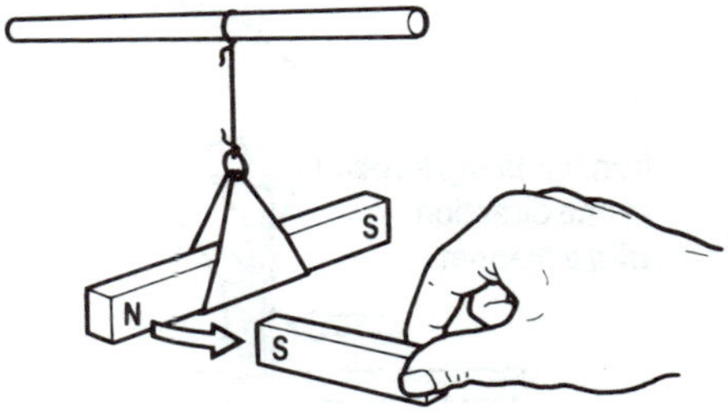

6 If we now move the second magnet far away, the suspended magnet will turn to another direction. This shows that it is still affected by another magnet.

Which magnet do you think that is? The earth

7 Do you think that the magnet will turn to lie (east-west, north-south)? (The sun sets in the west and rises in the east so we can work out which is east and west and north and south). Underline the right answer.

[8–12]
The Earth is round and spins on an imaginary axis. (You can make a model by pushing a knitting needle through an orange and spinning the orange round the knitting needle.) We call the two ends of the axis the north pole and the south pole.

The end of the magnet which is attracted towards the north pole is called the north pole of the magnet.

8 The other end of the magnet is called the south pole

So if we suspend the two magnets we can mark the ends N-pole and S-pole, according to the direction in which they are pointing.

9 We can now test whether N-poles are attracted to each other, or repelled. Which do you think it will be? Repelled

10–11 So we have discovered a rule of magnetism. N-poles are attracted to S-poles and repelled by N-poles

12 An extremely important navigating device depended on the discovery of magnets and the earth's magnetism and made the great voyages of such explorers as Vasco Da Gama, Christopher Columbus and Francis Drake possible. This was the magnetic compass

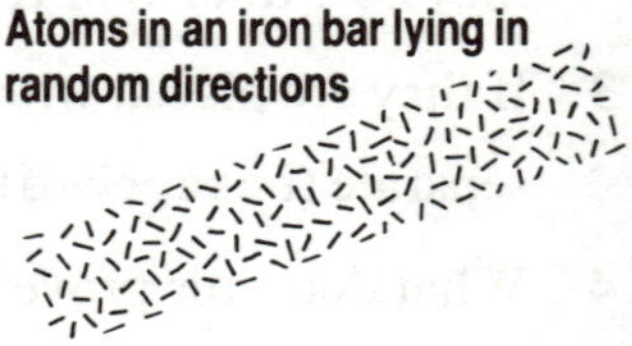

[13–16]
Each atom in a piece of iron or steel is a tiny magnet.

Ordinarily these atoms lie in random directions so that not much magnetism is apparent in the whole piece.

If we stroke a piece of iron or steel, such as a nail, with a magnet in one direction, the atoms in the nail tend to line up in that direction and its magnetic effect becomes much stronger – we will have made another magnet.

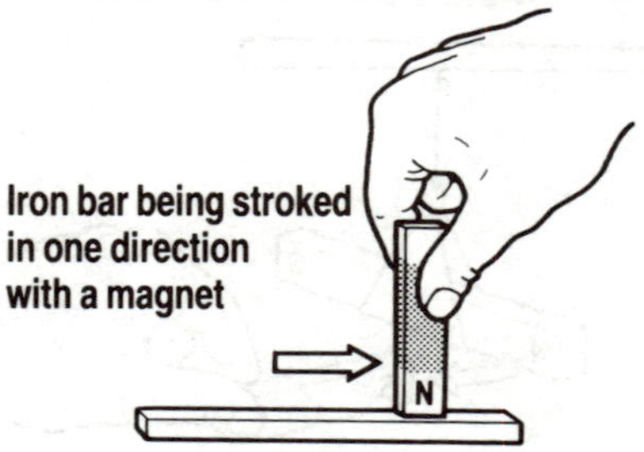

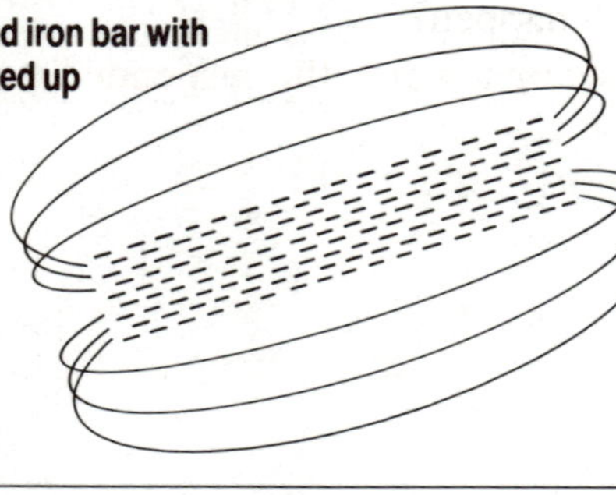

Similarly, we can destroy the magnetic effect by treating the iron or steel in such a way that the atoms are shaken up and become random again. Hammering or dropping the magnet, especially when heated, will tend to weaken its effect.

The nature of the magnetic effect can easily be seen if we take a magnet and some small particles of iron, such as iron filings.

If we lay the magnet on a piece of paper, sprinkle iron filings over the paper and tap the paper, the iron filings will arrange themselves in a pattern, with the strongest lines of filings running between the poles.

These mark the lines of force where the magnetic influence is strongest.

The atoms of very few substances behave as tiny magnets and show a magnetic effect.

Iron, and steel, which is mainly iron, as well as nickel and cobalt are the only **magnetic** substances. All others such as wood, plastics, glass and aluminium are **non-magnetic**.

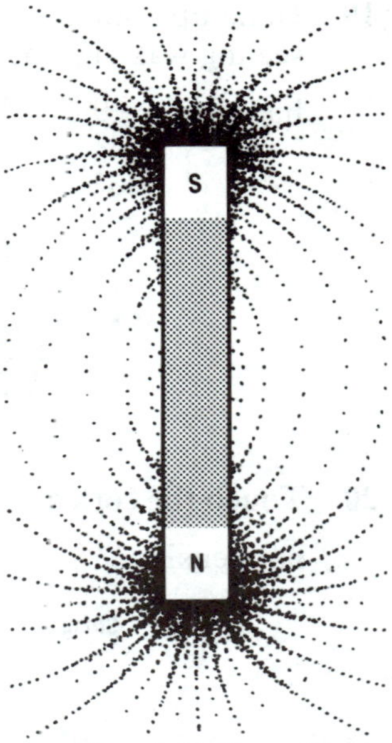

Iron filings in the lines of force around a magnet

13 Why does an ordinary nail not behave as a magnet? Because the atoms are pointing in random directions

14 What happens when a nail is stroked in one direction with a magnet? The atoms line up in one direction

15 Why do iron filings arrange themselves to show the lines of magnetic force? Because they are magnetic

16 Would copper filings or sawdust show the lines of magnetic force? No

Electricity in nature

[17–22]
Over 2500 years ago, a Greek philosopher called Thales found that if he rubbed a special kind of stone with fur, it became able to attract small pieces of fluff or feather. He called the stone, which we now call amber, **electron**.

17 If you comb your hair with a plastic comb and then hold the comb close to your hair, what happens? The hair is attracted to the comb

18 Have you ever noticed when pulling off nylon clothing over your head, on a dry day, that it crackles.

Why is this? Because sparks of electricity are produced

19 Hang up a small cork from a piece of thread and take a stick of sealing wax. Rub the sealing wax vigorously on your skirt or trousers and hold it close to the cork. What happens? The cork is attracted to the wax

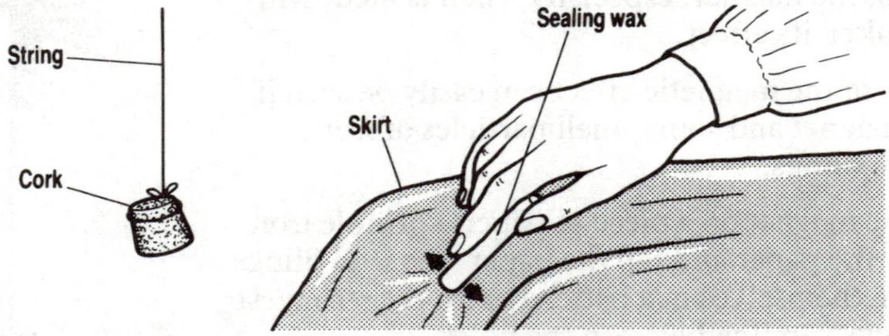

20 Touch the cork with the stick of wax and then hold it close to the cork again. What happens? The wax now repels the cork

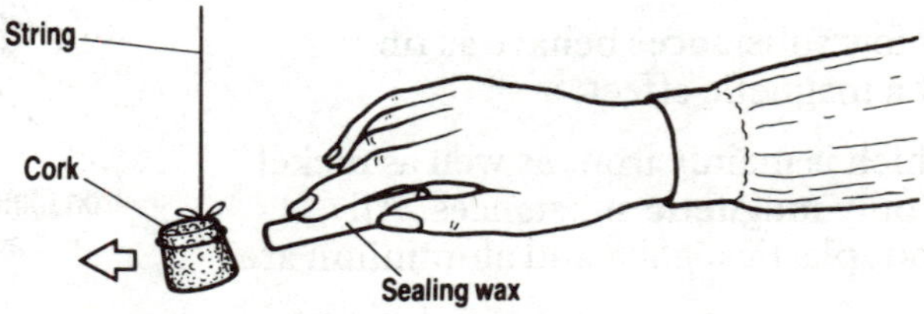

21 Why do you think that the result was different?
The wax and the cork now have the same charge

22 Did something get transferred from the cork to the wax? Yes – electrons

Rubbing some objects such as amber and plastics with fur or hair causes electric charges to build up on the surface of the object. This can be explained as follows.

[23–27]
All material things are made up from atoms which are very, very small.

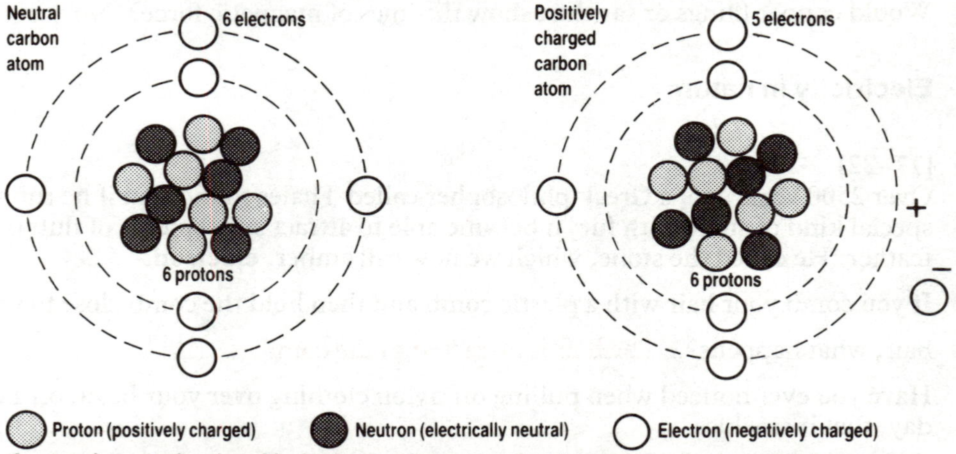

An atom in neutral and positively charged states showing the nucleus of neutrons and protons surrounded by orbiting electrons in neutral and positively charged states

All atoms have two main parts. There is the **nucleus** at the centre of the atom which is made up from two kinds of very small particle – **neutrons** and **protons**.

The nucleus is surrounded by some even smaller particles called **electrons**, which circle the nucleus rather like the planets circle the sun.

Neutrons and protons have almost the same **mass** but electrons have almost no mass.

Mass is the amount of matter in an object. This is not the same thing as the **weight** of an object which is the **force on an object due to the force of gravity** on its mass.

The amount of matter in an object will always be the same – its mass will be constant, but its weight will vary if the force of gravity varies.

A man who weighs 150 kilograms on the earth will weigh very much less than this on the moon, and nothing at all in space away from the Earth's gravity, but his mass is still 150 kilograms.

The kind of atom, whether it is iron, gold or oxygen, for example, depends on the number of neutrons and protons in its nucleus.

Consequently, atoms of heavy substances such as iron or gold have more neutrons and protons than atoms of light substances such as oxygen or carbon.

The protons in the nucleus of the atom carry what we call a positive charge, but the neutrons have no charge. Electrons carry what we call a negative charge.

Normally, atoms do not carry a charge which means that, the number of electrons circling the nucleus must equal the number of protons in the nucleus.

23 Will a heavy substance have more electrons than a light one? Yes

Underline the correct answers:

24 The mass of an atom is concentrated in the nucleus. (true, false)

25 The electrons of an atom are likely to be more easily displaced from the atom than the neutrons or protons. (true, false)

26 Can we see atoms? No

27 Do atoms show a charge under normal circumstances? No

[28–30]

When we rub the surface of a suitable material, such as amber, with fur, some of the electrons of the amber atoms are dragged off onto the fur.

The fur then has these extra electrons and becomes negatively charged while the amber atoms have lost some electrons and, as they are left with a surplus of protons, become positively charged.

These positively charged atoms then attract electrons from other things such as pieces of fluff or feathers and this is what causes the attractive force.

We do not really understand the nature of electric charges but we do know that positively charged things attract negatively charged ones, and that similar charges repel each other.

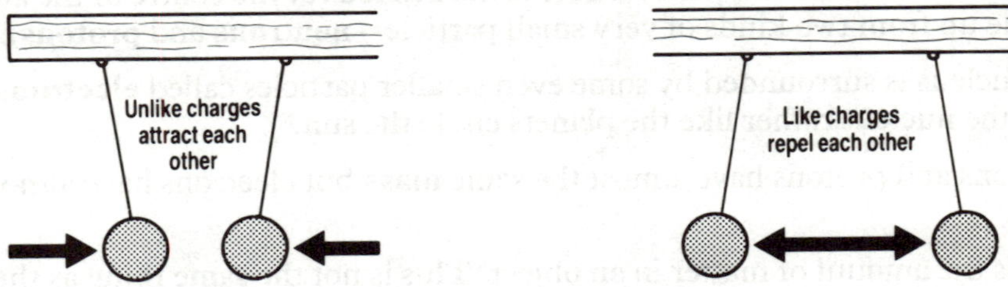

28 What might happen if atoms become positively charged and come near to some negatively charged fluff?

The atoms would attract the fluff

29 If a glass rod is rubbed with a piece of silk it becomes negatively charged. Has it lost or gained electrons? It has gained electrons

30 What do you think happens to the electrons when the glass rod is rubbed with silk?

Electrons from the silk become attached to the glass

Most of these experiments were first made many years ago and in 1646 a British scientist called Thomas Browne suggested that this force should be called **electricity**, after the Greek name for amber which was electron.

Many machines were devised to gather and store electrical charges of this kind and some of them could produce enough charge to make big sparks and flashes, but none of this electrical energy could be made useful to us.

We can see and hear this kind of electricity on a grand scale when we experience a thunderstorm.

[31–37]
Fill in the blanks using the words in this list:

touched thundercloud electricity ground conducted wire spark

Nearly 250 years ago, an American scientist called Benjamin Franklin made an experiment to try to prove that lightning was caused by ...electricity...

He flew a kite with a silk thread instead of a string, and with a ...wire... serving as the tail. He fixed a metal key to the silk thread where he could reach it.

He flew the kite up into a ...thundercloud... and then held his finger close to the key.

A ...spark... jumped across the gap between his finger and the key.

Each time he flew the kite up into a thundercloud he ...touched... the key and produced a spark.

This proved that the thunderclouds were charged with electricity and that some of this charge was ...conducted... down the thread and discharged to earth with a spark when Franklin, who was standing on the ...ground... touched the key.

[38–40]

38 Would you think such an experiment was dangerous? ...Yes...

Lightning can pass from one cloud to another or from a cloud to ground.

39 As a result of his experiment, Benjamin Franklin invented a device which has protected many tall buildings from damage from lightning. This is called a

...lightning conductor...

Even so, on average about twenty people a day are killed by lightning, throughout the world.

40 If the flash of light is the spark caused by a lightning discharge, what would you think thunder is? ...The sound of the spark...

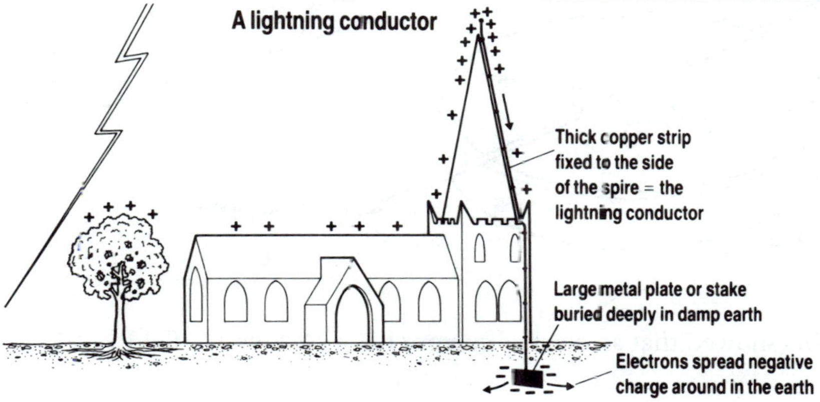

Making use of electricity

[41–47]
Although electricity and magnetism had been known about for a long time, the practical use of electrical energy awaited a more complete understanding of its nature.

Above all it depended on the discovery of a useful, reliable and controllable **source** of the mysterious power. Remember that nothing was known about atoms and electrons then!

One scientist who contributed greatly was an Italian, Count Volta (1745–1727) who invented the first practical battery.

He had been experimenting with various bits of metal dipped into salt solutions and finally made a stack of copper and zinc plates separated by sheets of cloth soaked in salt solution.

Then, in 1820, a Danish scientist Hans Christian Oersted discovered that the electric current from Volta's battery flowing through a wire would make a compass needle move.

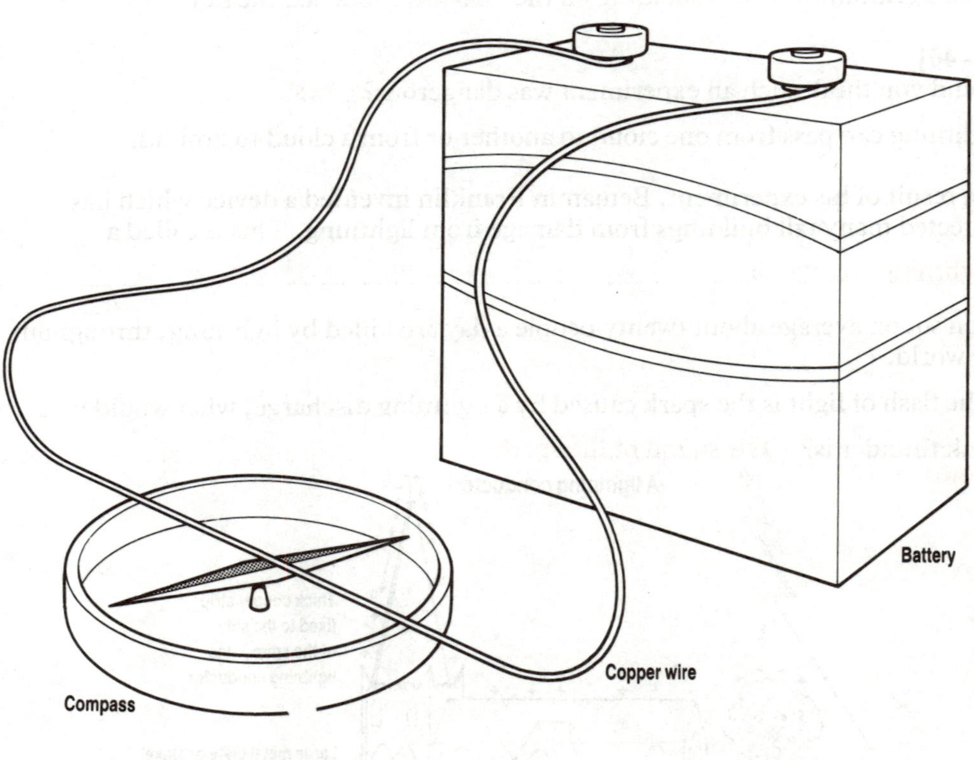

41 This showed that an electric current has a ....magnetic.... field.

Two years later the Frenchman André Ampère learnt that two wires that are carrying electric current attract and repel each other just like magnets.

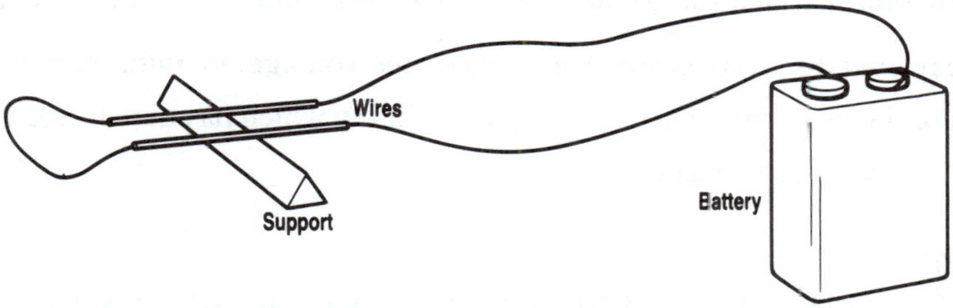

42 He had discovered (electric light, electromagnetism, that wires carry electric currents). Underline the correct answer.

Following on from these new observations, Michael Faraday succeeded in showing that moving a magnet inside a coil of wire made an electric current flow.

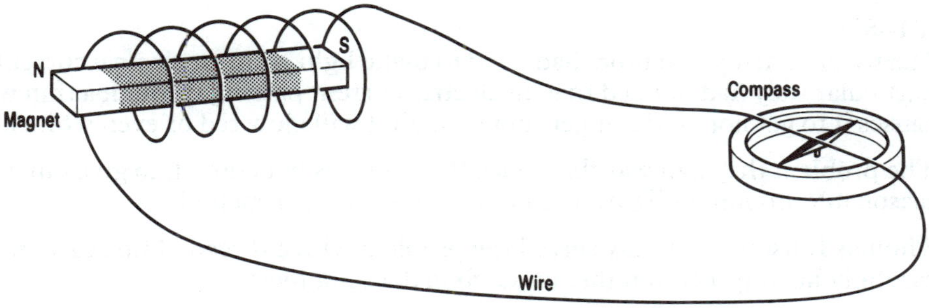

43 These experiments proved that magnetism could be converted into electricity

44 and electricity into magnetism,

45 they also showed how electrical energy could be made from mechanical energy and pointed the way to the first electric generator;

–47 and how mechanical energy could be produced from electricity in the electric motor

[48–53]
Fill in the blanks using the words in this list:

mechanical current magnets attract electricity generator

The discovery that moving magnets could produce an electric current lead to numerous inventors devising ways to mechanically move the magnets to produce a steady electric current and so the electric generator or **dynamo** was conceived, which could convert mechanical energy into electricity.

At the same time, the discovery that wires carrying an electric current could produce a magnetic field and so ...attract... magnetic materials gave rise to the **electric motor** which could convert electricity back into ...mechanical... energy.

These related discoveries, which are called **electromagnetic induction** were the origin of the modern ...electricity... supply industry which has transformed the world we live in so dramatically.

[54–60]
Here is a list of common electrical appliances. Underline those that use an electric motor:

drill	kettle	radiant heater	toothbrush	freezer
vacuum cleaner	television	digital watch	calculator	razor
cassette recorder	radio	typewriter		

[61–65]
Meanwhile, many inventors had tried to make light from an electric current. In particular they had noticed that an electric current passing through a thin wire causes it to get hot, and if it gets hot enough it will glow red or even white hot.

The problem they had was that, once the wire was hot enough to give out a reasonable amount of light, it either burnt through or melted.

Thomas Edison eventually solved the problem with a thread of fine carbon made by carefully heating a cotton thread. Carbon does not melt.

He reasoned that the thread could not burn away if there was no oxygen to make it burn, so he enclosed the carbon thread or **filament** in a glass bulb from which almost all the air had been removed.

The electric light bulb has since been improved by using a thin filament of tungsten wire, instead of the carbon. Tungsten is a metal which melts at an extremely high temperature.

Instead of simply removing most of the air in the glass bulb, it is all replaced with a gas called argon which does not react chemically with the hot filament and so prevents it from burning.

61 What causes the filament of a light bulb to get hot? ...The electric current...

62–63 Why did most filament materials tried by the inventors fail?

They ...melted... or ...burned...

64 Why could they not use copper as a filament? ...Copper would melt...

65 Why do you think that these lamps are called incandescent lamps?

...The light comes from the filament glowing white hot...

[66–70]
Fill in the blanks using the words in this list:

energy	**device**	**steam**	**conducted**	**socket**
generator	**wires**	**switch**	**boil**	**burned**

Electricity as we usually encounter it, is a form of ....energy.... generated at the power station.

Fuel is ....burned...., the heat is used to ....boil.... water to make ....steam.... and this is used to drive a turbine which turns a ....generator....

The generator produces electricity which is ....conducted.... to homes and factories along ....wires.... which we usually call power cables.

In our homes, the power ....socket.... allows us to connect with a source of energy.

How that energy is used depends on what device we attach.

We can get heat, light, drive machines, ring bells, hear music or see pictures according to the ....device.... we use. The energy is always ready and waiting for the turn of a ....switch....